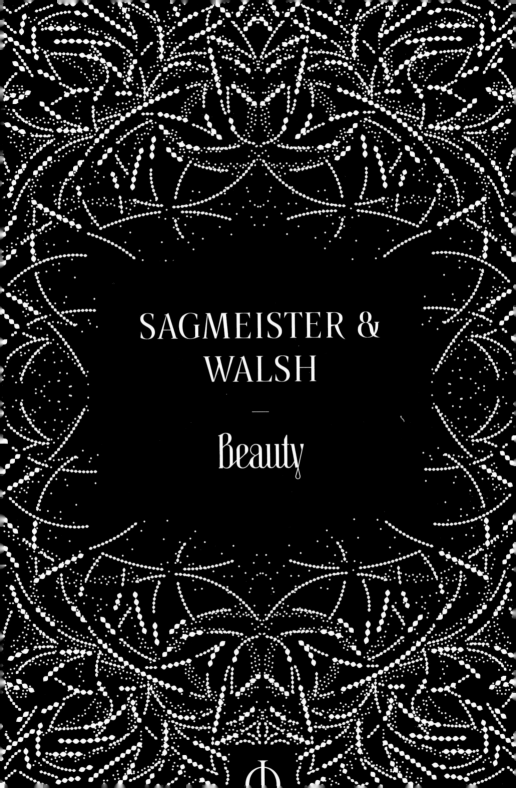

SAGMEISTER & WALSH

—

Beauty

INTRODUCTION TO BEAUTY

—

WHAT IS BEAUTY?

—

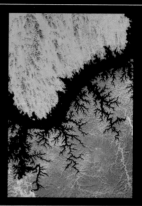

A SHORT HISTORY OF BEAUTY

—

EXPERIENCING BEAUTY

—

Introducti

to Beauty

The use of the word beauty *has declined over time within all books digitized by Google.*

Frequency of use of the word *beauty*

1800 1820 1840 1860 1880 1900 1920 1940 1960 1980 2000

B eauty as the height of aesthetic achievement has fallen out of favor. In the design world today, most respected practitioners claim not to be interested in it. Artists avoid it so as not to have their work labeled decorative or commercial. One can leaf through stacks of architecture books without seeing the term mentioned. At one time a universal aspiration, the pursuit of beauty came to a crash landing at the beginning of the twentieth century.

Since then, design schools have proselytized modernist principles, which privilege uniformity, the grid, rectangular compositions, and a preference for black, white, and beige. The approach to designing buildings, products, and graphics became purely analytical, the choice of materials entirely rational, the goal exclusively functional. Architects and designers often went to such extremes that they wound up designing everything with a psychotic sameness. Housing blocks built in the 1950s were dynamited decades later, unable to perform the single function for which they were created: providing human habitation.

This is not to say that Modernism doesn't deserve some credit—its tenets changed the way we think about and live in the world. In the right hands, its clean lines and reduced compositions can be incredibly gorgeous. Over time, however, its limitations have only become more pronounced. The principles fail to communicate anything distinctly individual—personality, uniqueness, emotion—and often have a crushing and negative effect on contemporary imagination. The essence of the problem lies in the radical misconception that beauty is old-fashioned, somehow embarrassing, and simply not a respectable goal for today's creatives.

We believe this rejection of beauty is utterly stupid. We'll demonstrate why by sharing our historical research on the philosophy of beauty. We'll consult with scientific advisers from the world of empirical aesthetics and conduct surveys to establish what people find beautiful. We'll use this information to prove that there is nothing superficial about beauty—far from it. Beauty means reaching beyond what just works or what is simply pretty. Beauty is the dose of humanity that makes our lives better. Beautiful works are not only more joyful, they also function much, much better.

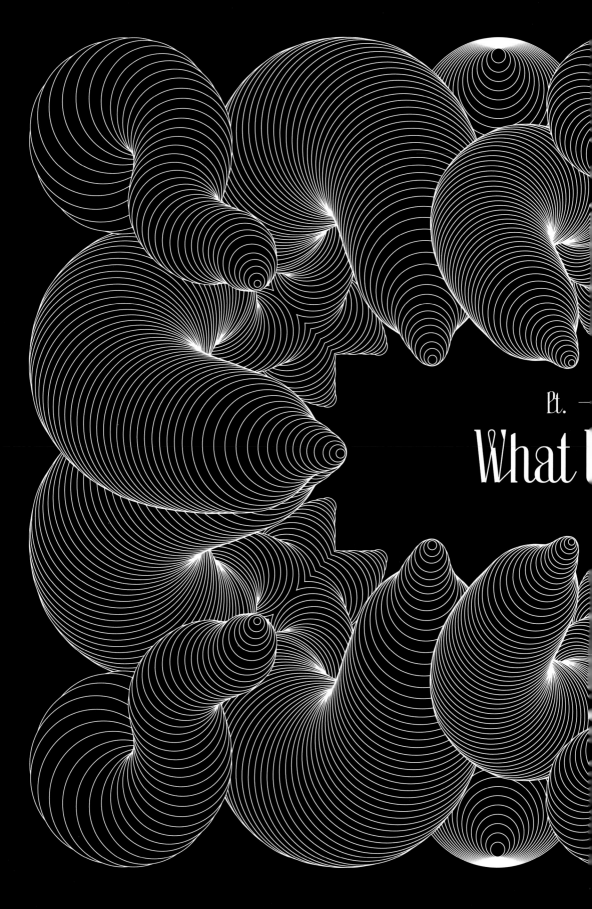

Pt. —

What

— I

eauty

AS designers, we became interested in studying beauty for practical reasons. Our ambitions weren't lofty; we simply wanted to increase the functionality of our designs. Our experience in the design studio has taught us that whenever we take form seriously—whenever we spend many hours perfecting the appearance of a design—it inevitably turns out to work much better. Mango juice sold in greater volume in India, concepts for museum branding were accepted and adopted faster by boards, and we're convinced that the content of our documentary *The Happy Film* resonated with audiences because we tried to make it look as good as possible.

Designers, architects, and artists can have a real impact on the quality of our lives and our environments, from the paper band holding our chopsticks together to the porcelain holder on which they rest, the tablecloth, the room containing the table, the building housing the restaurant, the street, the neighborhood, and the plan for the city. Everything is designed.

This can be done beautifully, or not. It is well worth our time to execute our environments with love, intelligence, care—and beauty.

We began to suspect that people feel differently in a beautiful environment. And we started to notice that they behave differently, too. So it seemed well worth our while to try to figure out what beauty really is.

"We Find Beauty in Something Done Well."[1]
–

American philosopher Denis Dutton posits that all well-executed human achievement could be described as beautiful. The beautiful goal in a soccer match or a fine musical composition is rightfully admired as an action performed at the highest level: "From Lascaux to the Louvre to Carnegie Hall, human beings have a permanent, innate taste for virtuoso displays [in the arts]."[2]

The same holds true for a mathematical equation. If a formula is right, it will also be elegant and beautiful. Nobel Prize–winning physicist Richard Feynman expressed it concisely: "You can recognize truth by its beauty and simplicity."[3]

The desire for beauty is part of what makes us human: cave paintings in Chauvet.

American mathematician George David Birkhoff went so far as to create a beauty formula in the beginning of the twentieth century: the measurement of beauty (M) equals a ratio of organization (O) to complexity (C). $M = O/C$. He believed beauty exists in the sweet spot between order and chaos, and he cited examples in nature—like the branch system of trees or a bolt of lightning—in support of his theory. This fine balance between organization and complexity can be applied to human-made things as well. From jewelry design to the planning of an entire city, the perfect equilibrium, Birkhoff believed, would be gorgeous.[4]

Certain proportions have been deemed particularly beautiful. The golden ratio—also known as the golden section, the golden mean, or the Greek letter *phi*—has been incorporated into many buildings, including the Parthenon in Athens. Leonardo da Vinci called it "the divine proportion," and it was used to achieve balance in many Renaissance sculptures and paintings.

But historically there has been scant evidence that the golden ratio is actually preferred by most people. If we examine the

Designed by City Planner
Designed by Motion Designer
Designed by Architect
Designed by Car Designer
Designed by Landscape Architect
Designed by Product Designer
Designed by Interface Designer
Designed by Fashion Designer
Designed by Graphic Designer

images and frames of art throughout history, many do not follow the proportions of the golden ratio.[5]

We posted our own survey on Instagram, and the rectangle designed according to the proportions of the golden ratio *did* come in first. We repeated the survey a couple of months later, and although only 17 percent were repeat voters, the results were the same: the golden ratio rectangle received 30 percent of the "most beautiful" votes, compared to around 23 percent for the other three rectangles.

So, it seems da Vinci was right after all: the golden ratio rules.

Is Beauty in the Object, or in the Mind?
▬

The question of whether or not beauty is intrinsic to the thing itself or determined by the eye of the viewer has been debated steadily—without resolution—since antiquity. Plato thought that the universe was gorgeous and would stay gorgeous even if no human being were there to witness it. Thus, the beauty of the universe must be inherent within it. He also thought that if something was beautiful, it was also true.

But later scholars frequently argued that beauty was not inherent in the object. David Hume wrote, "Beauty is no quality in things themselves: it exists merely in the mind which contemplates them."[6] Others believed beauty was conferred by its association with other things: whiteness was deemed beautiful because of its association with purity, the majesty of mountains with the power of the gods.*

Stendhal famously called beauty "only the *promise* of happiness."[7]

Friedrich Nietzsche went much further and viewed our existence in this world through the lens of an "aesthetic phenomenon." He thought the world was so awful that art is the only element that prevents us from killing ourselves: "Truth is ugly. We possess *art* lest we *perish* of the truth."[8] So while Plato equated beauty and truth, Nietzsche wanted to fight truth with beauty, which allows for the possible aesthetic power of the ugly. In a similar way, we can find joy in listening to dissonant music, where the tension increases the enjoyment of a beautiful passage. Humans look for tension to avoid boredom and seek the loud, the sudden, and the scary: "Anything that's exciting is pleasing."[9]

This still holds true in the creative departments of advertising agencies, where the main goal is an exciting idea, rather than a concept that's beautiful in its own right. When advertising banks on beauty, it tends to take the easy way out and feature human beauty (e.g., gorgeous models praising the advantages of one product or another) or natural beauty (when exotic locations are the focus of the pitch). Rarely do we see beauty as an intentionally and intelligently employed strategy, as it was in this British Benson & Hedges campaign from the 1980s.

Intentional beauty:
Benson & Hedges ads from the 1980s

WHICH OF THESE RECTANGLES
DO YOU THINK IS THE
MOST BEAUTIFUL?

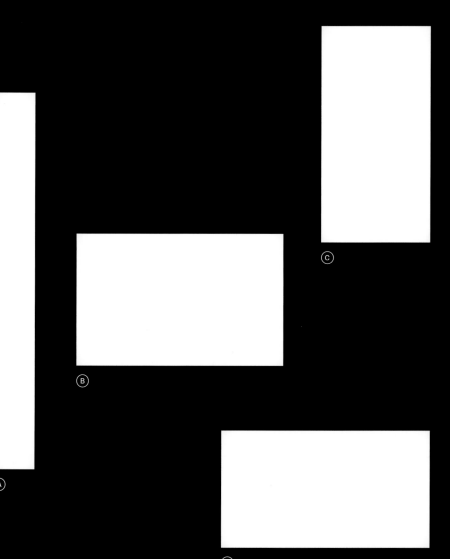

(A) 25%

883 *out of* 3,527

(B) 30%

1,052 *out of* 3,527

(C) 21%

739 *out of* 3,527

(D) 24%

853 *out of* 3,527

Beauty Made by Nature vs. Beauty Made by Humans

–

Georg Wilhelm Friedrich Hegel, the German philosopher, thought that beauty could only be achieved through the arts, not in nature. So a field of dandelions might be called beautiful, but a painting of a field of dandelions could somehow attain a higher form of beauty—an aesthetic triumph best understood by the intellect. We suspect Hegel would see the work of German artist Wolfgang Laib—who spends the months from early spring to early summer collecting dandelion, pine, and hazelnut pollen and then exhibits it carefully sieved into white-box galleries—as the most beautiful, since the intellect plays a more active role in understanding the work's gorgeousness.

Actual dandelions or painted dandelions: Which is the most beautiful?

Stefan recalls hiking in the Bregenzer Wald, a valley in western Austria close to where he grew up. He describes moments when the weather was perfect and he was in the right mood and came upon a new vista. Suddenly, he was in the presence of something sublime: a spectacular view at just the right moment— a rare moment of delight.

View of the Bregenzer Wald, close to where Stefan was born

Stefan often goes onto the roof of his building in New York, which overlooks the Manhattan skyline. When the mood and the weather are right, and the clouds conspire with the buildings to form a spectacular whole, he experiences a similar feeling to when he views the Bregenzer Wald, a scene of natural grandeur. Both visions produce moments of awe in response to their sheer magnificence.

View of New York City, where Stefan lives

If we compare historic Manahatta (the original name of the island when Peter Minuit

17

bought it from its Native American inhabitants) to contemporary Manhattan, Stefan believes that human intervention improved it remarkably; it's a much better looking place now.

Nature took about thirty million years to build the Austrian Alps, but it took New Yorkers only three hundred years to build the Manhattan skyline. Given how quickly the metropolis developed compared to the Austrian Alps, Stefan is ultimately more impressed with New Yorkers than with nature.

A Particular Amount of Complexity Is Best

—

Is it possible to consider beauty through the lens of science, or does identifying beauty scientifically have the effect of limiting our sensual and emotional appreciation of the experience?

Research has shown that we prefer environments that make sense to us, places that are easy to read, those with which we are in some way familiar. Psychologists Alex Forsythe and Noel Sheehy write, "We seek information and understanding and are predisposed to environments that are both interesting (complex) but also coherent (offering a degree of involvement that makes sense). Humans seek out a mixture of coherence and legibility (for understanding), but for exploration we prefer complexity with a degree of obscurity or mystery."[10]

Mathematician Benoit Mandelbrot demonstrated in 1975 that forms considered to be complete messes (i.e., perceived as having no underlying structure), like coastlines and clouds, actually contain a high degree of order.[11] He was able to recreate the complexity of a coastline following perfectly simple rules. He called these structures fractals. Fractals determine the form of mountains, rivers, plants, and animals, as well as sounds, like rain and waterfalls. Although the forms at first seem chaotic, they fall into a mathematical sequence that does indeed make sense.

Fractals at different degrees of complexity

Human beings usually prefer images that fall within the 1.3 to 1.5 fractal dimension, regardless of whether they are created by nature (coastlines or clouds), artists (Jackson Pollock's drip paintings), or mathematics.[12] We do seem to prefer a very particular level of complexity. In fact, there is solid evidence that the viewing of fractal patterns can reduce stress.[13]

We Love the Savanna but Lie on the Beach and Visit the Mountains

—

According to a seminal study published in 1982 by psychologists John D. Balling and John H. Falk, when it comes to choosing favorite landscapes, children are drawn to savanna-like environments. These are characterized by a path leading toward the horizon, some water close by, and terrain populated by midsize trees with branches low to the ground. According to evolutionary psychologists, we've inherited this preference from our prehistoric ancestors, who found this landscape to be the ideal environment for survival: the open vistas make predators easy to spot, and the presence of water and a path toward the horizon support sustainable life. The scattering of trees

DO YOU THINK IS THE MOST BEAUTIFUL?

Ⓐ

Ⓑ

 16%

613 out of 3,707

(B) 48%

1,771 out of 3,707

(C) 36%

with low branches offers an opportunity to climb up easily should danger arise and to see without being seen. The savanna hypothesis is particularly true for children who haven't been as exposed to contemporary cultural preferences as adults. It also helps explain why most parks around the world mimic, in many distinct ways, a savanna-like environment, with wide-open grass spaces and midsize trees featuring lateral branches.

Evolutionary psychology, of course, offers only partial explanations, and we would assume that our cultural and environmental influences sometimes supersede our evolutionary foundation. When we look at the locations in which people choose to spend their holidays, the savanna is not, it turns out, the biggest natural attraction: beaches and mountains are more popular. We polled our Instagram community, and almost four thousand people responded: the preferred landscape is mountainous. The savanna came in second, and rather surprisingly, the beach ended up as a distant third.

We had a statistician among our Instagram followers, and he took it upon himself to splice this data geographically. People from Germany and France preferred the savanna, and those in the Netherlands showed a strong preference for the mountains; so some desire for novelty, for a landscape that differs from one's own, also seems to play a role. It would appear that in this case, the grass is greener on the other side: we find most beautiful what we do not have.

Beauty and Sustainability
-

True beauty is an excellent strategy for long-term survival in architecture and design. One of the reasons the Pantheon has survived for two thousand years and wasn't razed (like so many other great buildings, in order to make room for new architecture) is its incredible beauty. Yes, its bronze roof was melted down by Gian Lorenzo Bernini to create the baldachin over the altar in St. Peter's Basilica, but the structure of the building itself is alive and well.* It has been in continuous use for over two millennia.

Many historical artifacts that we now admire in museums have survived for the same reason. Generations found them worthy of preservation, repair, and protection.

Stefan's briefcase:
a possible strategy for sustainability

Even on a much smaller scale, objects of beauty inspire us to take care of them. Stefan's thirty-year-old briefcase, given to him as a gift, is a perfect example. He loved it right away, and whether the threads became loose, the clasp needed reinforcement, or the inside required refitting, he never considered replacing it—he always has it repaired. The leather has become all the more beautiful with wear.

Beauty = Human
-

Dr. Helmut Leder runs the Empirical Visual Aesthetics Lab in Vienna, one of the leading institutes for visual aesthetics in psychology today. He studies the effects of beauty and ugliness on our feelings and our behavior. He readily complains about the scarcity of authoritative research in his field. He claims beauty fell out of favor not only in the arts, design, and architecture disciplines during the twentieth century, but also in psychology.

In one of his studies, titled "An Island of Stability," he and his colleagues researched people suffering from Alzheimer's disease.[14]

* Another part of the roof was used to make cannons.

WHAT IS BEAUTY?

Patients in the study were shown a number of paintings—in a different order for each patient. They were then asked to select the most beautiful, the second most beautiful, and so on. The patients had no trouble putting the images into a sequence from most to least beautiful.

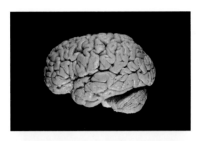

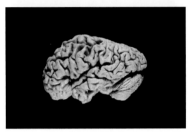

Healthy brain vs. brain afflicted with Alzheimer's

Two weeks later, Leder reconvened the study with the same participants and once again explained the task at hand, using the same group of paintings. Although the patients did not remember the paintings, or that they had performed this task before, nearly every patient put the images into the same sequence he or she had created two weeks earlier. We can infer from Leder's results that, even when memory functions are dissipated, an ability

Patients easily sequence paintings from most to least beautiful.

to look for and recognize beauty—however subjective—persists.

We Recognize Beauty Unconsciously
—

Leder and his colleague Dr. Gernot Gerger created an experiment in which they equipped participants with a measuring device placed on the facial muscle that controls smiling and frowning. The device picks up very subtle movements in these muscles.[15]

In the experiment, they presented participants with a set of images in a random sequence. This set was previously tested, and participants had determined some of the images to be clearly beautiful or not beautiful. The images were shown for only 1/25 of a second—too short a time to consciously identify the "beautiful" images—and when asked about them, the participants were often not aware they'd seen the images at all. However, according to the muscle measuring device, all of the participants' smiling muscles contracted when the beautiful images were shown. One can deduce that the unconscious mind recognizes beauty and responds positively, even if the conscious mind is unaware of it.

When we look at large audiences visiting New York's Museum of Modern Art or the Louvre in Paris, it seems they are attracted to pleasant and positive pieces. The exhibition spaces featuring Henri Matisse's works in New York, for example, or the *Mona Lisa* in Paris, are always crowded. Although laypeople seem to be drawn to beautiful work, art experts seem to be attracted to more difficult work—pieces that are more visually challenging, provocative, or even disgusting.

In another study, using the same facial-muscle measuring device, Leder and his colleagues worked with Dr. Norbert Schwarz, a world-leading social psychologist and professor at the University of Southern California.[16] They set out to determine whether or not the unconscious mind would reveal different opinions than those expressed in public. They wanted to test whether art experts indeed experience positive emotions when exposed to provocative, difficult, and possibly even disgusting artworks, and whether this emotion coincides with a physical reaction or reveals their admiration to be purely intellectual.

Dr. Leder's Empirical Visual Aesthetics Lab in Vienna

Artworks portraying "negative" content prompted frowns among the experts—as they did with the nonexperts—while the beautiful images elicited smiles. However, when asked to evaluate the artworks, the art experts liked the negative artworks more than the nonexperts liked them. So, although the experts' frowning muscles indicated negative emotions, this reaction did not diminish the experts' appreciation the way it did for the nonexperts. In another study, Leder and his colleagues found an additional difference between the experts and nonexperts: while most people prefer symmetry, people who study art prefer asymmetry.[17]

This is also true for simple compositions:

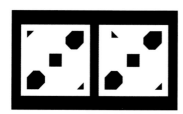

Which of these images do you think is more beautiful?

Laypeople prefer the symmetrical composition on the left, while experts prefer a slight asymmetrical ingredient.

We Do Like What We Know
—

Schwarz also conducted groundbreaking research concerning beauty and fluency.[18] He states that "when an object is easy to perceive, people evaluate it as more beautiful than when it is difficult to perceive."[19] The more effortlessly an observer can process an object, the more beautiful she would perceive that object to be.

Historically, the notion of beauty as intrinsic to a given object, rather than determined by each individual observer, gave rise to numerous efforts by theorists dating back to Plato to identify the features that made the object visually appealing. Prominent among these features are simplicity, symmetry, balance, clarity, contrast, and proportion.

Schwarz writes that these essential features have one thing in common: "They are likely to facilitate processing of the stimulus. From this perspective, visual appeal does not reside in attributes of the object of appreciation but in the processing experience of the perceiver: an object is appealing when it is fluently processed, which is a function of stimulus, perceiver, and context variables."[20] So we find something beautiful depending on how easy it is for us to understand, how familiar we are with its form, and in what context we experience it. Schwarz demonstrates that people are more willing to explore new things when the surroundings are familiar.

Similarly, Polish-born American social psychologist Dr. Robert Zajonc showed in the 1960s that the more often a viewer was exposed to something, and the more familiar it became, the more appealing it became. He suggested an evolutionary explanation for why a familiar stimulation was preferred: "If it is familiar, it has not eaten you...yet."[21]

The human face is the most popular image featured on magazine covers.

The link between an image's familiarity and the likelihood that we will find it pleasing was borne out when we visited Amazon.com. Stefan gave a lecture to the design staff, and at the luncheon afterward, the conversation turned to the power of book cover images on the Amazon site. According to staffers, the book covers that receive the most clicks include images of the human face. In second place are covers with illustrations of pets, usually cats and dogs. It suddenly became clear why the vast majority of print magazines feature a face on the cover. Magazines depend on newsstand sales, so they feature what attracts us most: the human face.* Assuming Amazon's data is true, why would we stray from what we know works? If we only like what is familiar, why do we innovate at all? Why are we not still using stone axes? Leder also worked with the German professor of psychology Claus-Christian Carbon, and they were able to show that innovations are indeed perceived as irritating in the beginning, but they become more pleasing over time. When the end user feels secure, the effect is increased. Conversely, if the test is conducted in an irritating environment, this pleasing effect vanishes.[22]

Stefan's experiences in the music industry similarly reflect the human tendency toward the familiar. When business went into decline with the rise of Napster and digital downloads, music companies' desire to invest in groundbreaking graphic design declined. It became clear very quickly that when business was suffering, only safe work would be accepted.

How Beautiful Is That Mondrian?

Dr. Chris McManus, a research psychologist at the University College London, devoted much of his work to Piet Mondrian, one of the great twentieth-century artists. Mondrian's abstract compositions are carefully constructed, and we know from X-raying his paintings that he moved those lines around endlessly before settling on a composition.[23] He believed beauty was based on a balance of complementary forces, and that these forces represented a unity not only of the mind but also of the entire universe. In a study, McManus took a reproduction of a lesser-known Mondrian, one with which most of us are not readily familiar, and created a fake version, changing the composition slightly.[24] He wanted to find out if participants could distinguish between the original and the fake.

We have conducted this test in front of dozens of audiences, asking them to raise their hands to indicate votes for the real and fake versions, and roughly 85 percent of the people recognize the original every time. This is the case whether we run the experiment with European, American, Asian, or Australian audiences. In Mexico City, 100 percent of the audience identified the true Mondrian.

Beauty stands in a realm of its own. While it eludes an easy definition, people know it when they see it. Our prior experiences, as well as the context in which we see something, both play important roles in our aesthetic judgments. It also seems there is surprising agreement across cultures about what is beautiful and what is not.

Beauty is not something skin deep: it is part of what it means to be human.

ONE OF THESE MONDRIANS IS FAKE. CAN YOU PICK THE ORIGINAL?

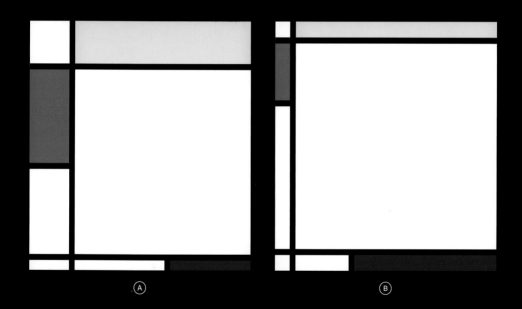

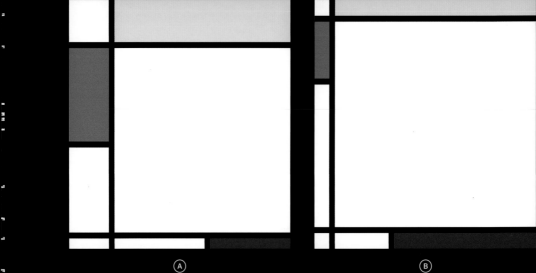

A

B

1. Denis Dutton, "A Darwinian Theory of Beauty" (TED2010, Long Beach, CA, February 12, 2010), https://www.ted.com/talks/denis_dutton_a_darwinian_theory_of_beauty.

2. Dutton, "A Darwinian Theory of Beauty."

3. Richard Feynman, The Character of Physical Law (Cambridge, MA: MIT Press, 1985), 171.

4. George David Birkhoff, Aesthetic Measure (Cambridge, MA: Harvard University Press, 1933).

5. Richard L. Gregory, "Aesthetics," in The Oxford Companion to the Mind, ed. Richard L. Gregory (New York: Oxford University Press, 2004), 10.

6. David Hume, "Of the Standard of Taste," in English Essays from Sir Philip Sidney to Macaulay, ed. Charles W. Eliot (New York: Collier, 1910), 215-36.

7. Stendhal [Marie-Henri Beyle], On Love (Plymouth, Great Britain: Mayflower, 1915), 56.

8. Aaron Ridley, "Perishing of the Truth: Nietzsche's Aesthetic Prophylactics," British Journal of Aesthetics 50, no. 4 (October 2010): 427-37.

9. Konrad Paul Liessmann, Schoenheit (Vienna: Facultas, 2009), 62.

10. Alex Forsythe and Noel Sheehy, "Is It Not Beautiful?" The Psychologist 24, no. 7 (July 2011): 504-7. What Forsythe and Sheehy describe is the theory of Kaplan and Kaplan (1987); see for example https://thepsychologist.bps.org.uk/volume-24/edition-7/it-not-beautiful.

11. Benoit Mandelbrot, Fractals: Form, Chance, and Dimension (New York: W. H. Freeman, 1977).

12. Richard P. Taylor and Branka Spear, "Fractal Fluency: An Intimate Relationship between the Brain and Processing of Fractal Stimuli," in The Fractal Geometry of the Brain, ed. Antonio Di Ieva, Springer Series in Computational Neuroscience (New York: Springer-Verlag, 2016), 485-96. A fractal dimension is a ratio providing a certain index of complexity.

13. Richard P. Taylor, "Reduction of Physiological Stress Using Fractal Art and Architecture," Leonardo 39, no. 3 (June 2006): 245-51.

14. Daniel Graham, Simone Stockinger, and Helmut Leder, "An Island of Stability: Art Images and Natural Scenes—But Not Natural Faces—Show Consistent Esthetic Response in Alzheimer's-Related Dementia," Frontiers in Psychology 4, no. 107 (March 2013), doi: 10.3389/fpsyg.2013.00107.

15. Gernot Gerger, Helmut Leder, Pablo P. L. Tinio, and Annekathrin Schacht, "Faces Versus Patterns: Exploring Aesthetic Reactions Using Facial EMG," Psychology of Aesthetics, Creativity, and the Arts 5, no. 3 (2011): 241-50.

16. Helmut Leder, Gernot Gerger, David Brieber, and Norbert Schwarz, "What Makes an Art Expert? Emotion and Evaluation in Art Appreciation," Emotion & Cognition 28, no. 6 (2014): 1137-47.

17. Helmut Leder, Pablo P. L. Tinio, David Brieber, et al., "Symmetry Is Not a Universal Law of Beauty," forthcoming in Empirical Studies of the Arts.

18. Rolf Reber, Norbert Schwarz, and Piotr Winkielman, "Processing Fluency and Aesthetic Pleasure: Is Beauty in the Perceiver's Processing Experience?" Personality and Social Psychology Review 8, no. 4 (November 2004): 364-82.

19. Norbert Schwarz, "Of Fluency, Beauty, and Truth: Inferences from Metacognitive Experiences," in Metacognitive Diversity: An Interdisciplinary Approach (New York: Oxford University Press, 2017), 2.

20. Schwarz, "Of Fluency, Beauty, and Truth," 16.

21. Matthew Willcox, The Business of Choice: Marketing to Consumers' Instincts (Upper Saddle River, NJ: Pearson FT, 2017), 41.

22. Claus-Christian Carbon, Stella Färber, Gernot Gerger, Michael Forster, and Helmut Leder, "Innovation Is Appreciated When We Feel Safe: On the Situational Dependence of the Appreciation of Innovation," International Journal of Design 7, no. 2 (August 2013): 43-51.

23. Anna Martins, Cynthia Albertson, Chris McGlinchey, and Joris Dik, "Piet Mondrian's Broadway Boogie Woogie: Noninvasive Analysis Using Macro X-ray Fluorescence Mapping (MA-XRF) and Multivariate Curve Resolution-Alternating Least Square (MCR-ALS)," Heritage Science 4, no. 22 (December 2016), doi: 10.1186/s40494-016-0091-4.

24. Ian Christopher McManus, "Experimenting with Mondrian: Comparing the Method of Production with the Method of Choice" (lecture, Sixth International Conference on Design Computing and Cognition, University College London, June 2014).

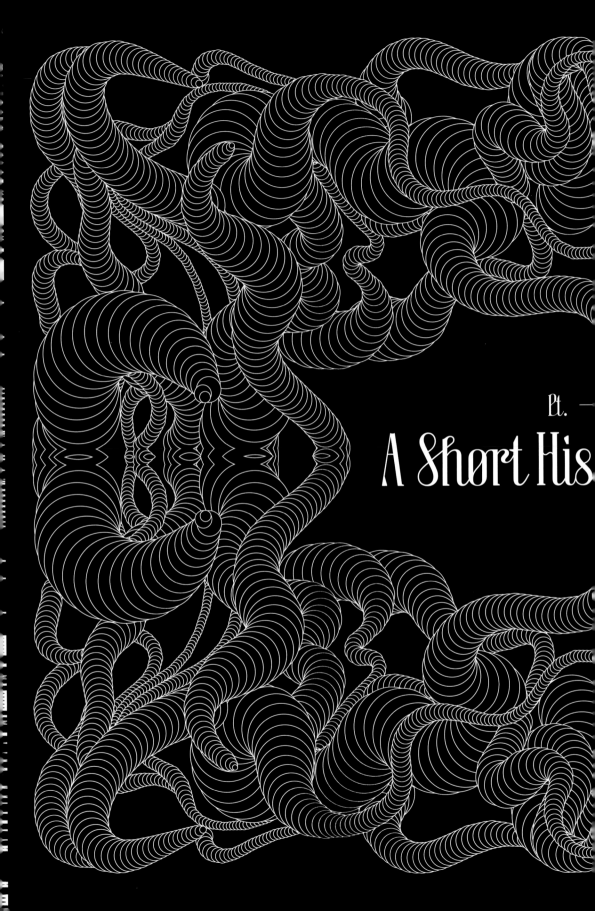

Pt. —

A Short His

— II

y of Beauty

32

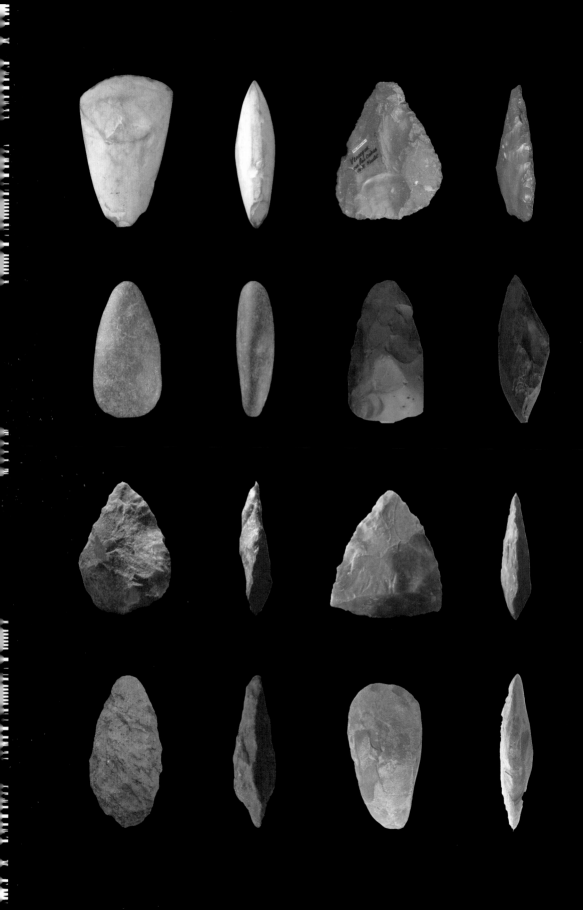

Beauty has played a significant role over the course of history. Even before we were technically human—before we were *Homo sapiens*—we were already making decisions inspired by aesthetic considerations. Since then, beauty has been embraced by human culture—from Sumeria and Assyria to Greece and the Roman Empire and all the way to the end of the nineteenth century. It was only during the twentieth century that beauty was pushed to the side in favor of functionality.

Beautiful Tools

Humankind's first tool was the stone ax. We started making them more than one million years ago, and large numbers of these axes have been found in Asia, Europe, Africa, and the Americas. We used them before we had language, and even before we fully evolved into the human species (*Homo sapiens* came into being only about two hundred thousand years ago).

Surprisingly, many of these stone axes are perfectly symmetrical. From a functional point of view, there is no reason for this symmetry: you can kill that saber-toothed tiger just as well with an asymmetrical sharp stone. Philosopher Denis Dutton believes we made the axes symmetrical for aesthetic reasons, simply because we found them more pleasing.[1] In addition to the tool-size axes, Dutton points out that archaeologists have also discovered six-meter-tall symmetrical stones that have no apparent practical function: you can't lift them, you can't work with them, you cannot *do* anything with them. It's likely our ancestors simply wanted to impress someone—specifically, a potential partner: "Look, I made this!"

There's a reason that human beings regard symmetry as especially beautiful. In order to survive, our ancestors had to identify symmetrical repetitions (and interruptions to these repetitions) that occurred in their environment. For instance, detecting a hidden predator, or finding edible fruit, necessitated a sophisticated ability to spot patterns in the surroundings. In his 1871 lecture "On Symmetry," physicist and philosopher Ernst Mach suggested a connection between the survival of early humans, who were deft at spotting symmetrical repetition, and modern humankind's adoption of symmetrical repetition as one of the basic building blocks of all ornament.[2]

Plato and Socrates Talk in a Bar

The ancient Greeks were smitten by beauty perhaps more than any previous or subsequent society. Arguably, the most influential text from this time period on beauty comes from Plato's Socratic dialogues, in which he characterizes beauty as one of the ultimate values, together with truth and justice. In these dialogues, he states that if something is beautiful, it is also morally good.[3] Whatever is good is beautiful, whatever is beautiful is also good. Further, Plato goes on to equate beauty with truth and truth with beauty.

Subsequent generations across the disciplines have constructed theories meant to define beauty. Art historians have debated the definition, some positing a grand theory of beauty, which states that all beautiful works include objective and fundamental principles such as proportion, symmetry, and harmony.

Harmony combines different things into a working whole.

Tall, symmetrical stone with no practical function:
we made it because it was beautiful.

Beauty

=

Goodness

=

Truth

In Homer's telling, Harmonia was born to Ares, the god of war, and Aphrodite, the goddess of love (who was married to someone else). As the love child of two very different parents, Harmonia exemplified the credo, "To create harmony means to combine things that diverge from each other into a working whole."[4]

Light in one of its most transcendent expressions: the windows of Gothic cathedrals

Light, too, played an enormous role in Islamic and European art and architecture, based on the ancient belief that the sun is a god. Light finds its most transcendent expression in Gothic cathedrals and their colorful glass windows, as well as in the great Dutch paintings from the Golden Age.

**Beauty Applied in
Art and Architecture**

-

Several historical eras stand out for the value they placed on pursuing beauty—both its creation and its meaning. Not only did the Egyptians and Greeks see beauty as fundamental to the buildings and sculptures they created, but the Greeks went so far as to formalize a philosophy of beauty (Plato's ideas remain influential to this day). The Romans took many of these ideas and developed them further, experimenting with painted portraits, wall paintings, and novel building materials, such as concrete. The Roman architect Vitruvius wrote that successful architecture must combine elements of order, arrangement, proportion, symmetry, decor, and distribution.[5]

In the Middle Ages, beauty found its most exalted form in Gothic cathedrals. The longstanding notion that beauty is connected to something larger than ourselves—a spiritual ideal, a religious state, an expression of God—became reflected in the built environment. That shifted during the Renaissance, when the notion of the artistic genius as creator of beauty—Leonardo da Vinci and Michelangelo, for example—took center stage. Their egos followed accordingly. After Michelangelo's *Pietà* was placed in St. Peter's Basilica in Rome, the sculptor reportedly overheard a group of people discussing its beauty, and when one asked who made it, another answered, "Some guy from Milan." The Florentine Michelangelo was so upset that he sneaked into St. Peter's at night and added to the band around Mary: *Michaela[n]gelus Bonarotus Florentin[us] Facieba[t]* ("Michelangelo Buonarroti, from Florence, made this").

One of Stefan's favorite paintings is not da Vinci's *Mona Lisa* but his lesser-known work *Lady with an Ermine*, now hanging in its own room in the National Museum in Krakow, Poland. Stefan saw it last year, and while more glorious in the original, this printed reproduction does a fine job of depicting much of its formal mastery. The juxtaposition of the beautifully depicted Cecilia Gallerani and the strange animal in her arms, and the contrast of expressions on Gallerani's face and the animal's—all painted using the artist's signature *sfumato* technique, where he softens the edges with dark transparent glazes—combine into a gorgeous whole.

While we're talking about beautiful paintings, another favorite of ours is *St. Francis in*

Leonardo da Vinci,
Lady with an Ermine, c. 1489–90

the Desert at the Frick Collection in New York City. Even with the enormously high bar set by the Rembrandts, Vermeers, and Titians in the museum, Giovanni Bellini's masterpiece stands out. It depicts the saint in ecstasy, surrounded by a symbolic landscape.* Bellini's use of color and atmosphere is divine.

Giovanni Bellini,
St. Francis in the Desert, c. 1476–78

As an aside, when visiting the Frick, don't miss Jean-Auguste-Dominique Ingres's masterpiece, painted four hundred years after Bellini's St. Francis: the portrait of Louise de Broglie, *Comtesse d'Haussonville.* Ingres painted the color of her dress in the same hue

that was voted as the most beautiful shade of blue in our own Instagram survey (see p. 122).

The Nineteenth-Century Beauty Craze

The nineteenth century was obsessed with beauty. The idea that true beauty can only be expressed through the arts, and that art has no other function than to create beauty, was widespread. Artists such as the German painter Anselm Feuerbach dedicated their entire careers to it. Philosopher and Bloomsbury Group member G. E. Moore, who influenced fellow members T. S. Eliot, Virginia Woolf, and the rest of the Bloomsbury set, embraced the Greek theme of beauty as a moral value.

Meanwhile, French novelist and critic Théophile Gautier believed that if something worked, it couldn't be beautiful: function would drag beauty down into the gutter. He asked, "What is the most functional room in the house?" and came to the conclusion that it's the bathroom—with, of course, the toilet—hardly the most beautiful.[6]

Poets also glorified the idea of beauty, which is famously celebrated in John Keats's "Endymion":

> *A thing of beauty is a joy for ever:*
> *Its loveliness increases; it will never*
> *Pass into nothingness; but still will keep*
> *A bower quiet for us, and a sleep*
> *Full of sweet dreams, and health,*
> *and quiet breathing.*

The nineteenth century also saw the rise of the term *beaux arts* (*die schoenen Kuenste* in German). The "beautiful arts"—which included painting, sculpture, music, poetry, dance, architecture, and rhetoric—were clearly differentiated from the *artes liberales* (sciences) and *artes vulgares* (crafts).

The earlier practice of copying from nature and history became fashionable again as a

London purchased the painting for £630 in the nineteenth century, and it remains one of the museum's most gorgeous pieces.

of a Rolling Stones single. It was rejected, not because it was not beautiful enough but because of a song title change. The National Gallery in

* Bellini also painted another of our favorites in the history of art: the portrait of the Doge Leonardo Loredan. We proposed it for the design

Michelangelo, *Pietà*, 1499:
Michelangelo Buonarroti, from Florence, made this.

Artists like Anselm Feurbach dedicated their entire careers to beauty.

strategy for achieving beauty. As art historian Johann Joachim Winckelmann proposed in the eighteenth century, in a volume aptly titled *Reflections on the Imitation of Greek Works in Painting and Sculpture*, the only way for us to become inimitable is to imitate.[7]

Nineteenth-century artists produced replicas of Greek sculptures.

When copying Greek sculptures, artists in the nineteenth-century produced replicas out of white marble, unaware that these sculptures were originally painted in bright colors. This omission of color and ensuing glorification of white can be seen as one of the bridges leading to an almost complete absence of color in Modernism—a fear of color (chromophobia), and a reflexive preference for white or black.

Stealing Beauty
—

The power of the Austrian Empire, with Vienna as its center, reached its zenith in the nineteenth century. Emperor Franz Joseph decreed that the first district, which includes the elegant Ringstrasse, would be home to the most important institutions of the empire. The state opera house was built in fake Renaissance style, the city hall in faux Gothic, the Austrian Parliament in ersatz Greek, and the Burgtheater in pseudo-Baroque. The extra-wide, tree-lined boulevard was punctuated by parks and lined with opulent mansions. To embellish these private residences, inside and out, architects could turn to elaborate catalogues featuring examples of ornamentation from all periods of architectural history. While today it is not readily apparent which building is an original and which is a copy, Vienna's popularity with tourists owes much to the constructions built in the nineteenth century.

Nineteenth-century architectural details, ready to order

Yet when visiting museums containing nineteenth-century art, such as the Neue Pinakothek in Munich, we have been surprised by how few of the pieces truly speak to us. Considering that much of this work was created with beauty as its central goal, we are startled by our indifference to the works. The nineteenth century's single-minded pursuit of beauty seems to fall flat when viewed from today's perspective. Rather than achieving something close to beauty, many works come much closer to kitsch.

From today's perspective, many nineteenth-century artists achieved not beauty but something more readily associated with kitsch.

*To paraphrase
Johann Joachim Winckelmann:*

The only way
for us
to become
inimitable is to
imitate.

Ironically, as the strategy for achieving beauty through ornamentation continued to fall out of favor in the twentieth century—making way for purist goals focused exclusively on functionality and economy—a similar disconnect between goal and outcome emerged. So many of the projects created throughout the functionalists' golden period in the second half of the twentieth century—like public housing projects and airline emergency cards—were not successful. Nobody wanted to live in the former or to read the latter. Much of functionalism did not function.

VORTRAG
VERANSTALTET VOM AKAD.
ARCHITEKTEN VEREIN.

**ADOLF LOOS:
ORNAMENT
UND
VERBRECHEN.**

FREITAG, DEN 21. FEBRUAR 1913,
½ 8ʰ ABENDS IM FESTSAAL DES
ÖSTERR. ING. U. ARCH. VEREINES,
I. ESCHENBACHGASSE 9.
KARTEN ZU 5, 4, 3, 2, 1 K
BEI KEHLENDÖRFER
12. MÄRZ:
MISS LEVETUS: ALTENGL. KATHEDRALEN.
MITTE MÄRZ:
DR. HABERFELD: ÜBER ADOLF LOOS.

Adolf Loos believed that his time necessitated its own artistic expression.

Ornament, Crime, and Misdemeanors: Adolf Loos and the Bauhaus
-

Architect Adolf Loos despised the aesthetic stealing from the past that informed the strategies of many nineteenth-century creatives. He believed that the present necessitated its own artistic expression. The Machine Age had started, and relying solely on elements from the past was a travesty: "Every epoch had its own style, and ours alone should be denied one?"[8] In 1910, he gave a talk in which he argued that architects who forced craftspeople to add ornamentation to their work were criminal, as such activity was a waste of labor—it made the work fashionable, which then pushed it out of style more quickly. He also strongly opposed ornamenting the body: "There are prisons in which 80 percent of the inmates have tattoos. People with tattoos not in prison are either latent criminals or degenerate aristocrats."[9]

Loos also argued that simple designs would be more cost-effective to produce. But the idea that less-elaborate objects would be cheaper to manufacture was questionable from the beginning. Straight lines were difficult to achieve in mass production, as every irregularity became apparent immediately, while rich ornamentation was better able to hide flaws. As two bowls from 1846 and 1918 clearly show (see opposite page), simplicity was often harder to manufacture. The ornamental bowl was inexpensively made using a machine mold, while the simple one needed to be painstakingly constructed by hand, requiring many hours of manual labor in order to make it look like it was made by a machine.

Loos, who believed "lack of ornamentation [was] a sign of intellectual strength," worked in stark contrast to Josef Hoffmann and the

Loos's Haus am Michaelerplatz in Vienna: "the house without eyebrows"

The idea that creating a simple object is cheaper than a complex one was flawed from the beginning.

Anonymous, Basket, Vienna, 1846; silver, pressed and cast; machine-made, cheap

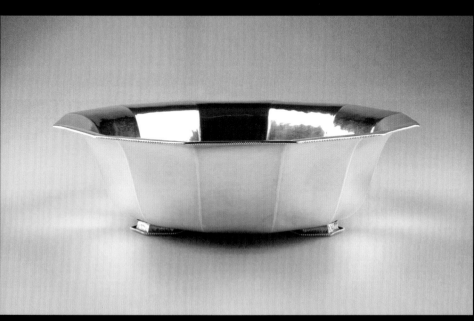

Josef Hoffmann, Silver Bowl, 1918; manufactured by Wiener Werkstätte, Vienna; handmade, expensive

c. 1550–1600

c. 1600

c. 1610

c. 1670

c. 1700

c. 1711

c. 1620

c. 1650

c. 1650

c. 1730

c. 1740

c. 1750

c. 1916–17

c. 1960

c. 2018

Beauty played an important role throughout human history. This changed significantly during the twentieth century.

Wiener Werkstätte, whose invention of new, contemporary ornaments he particularly despised.* As far as Loos was concerned, his Haus am Michaelerplatz didn't need any historic flourishes; it came to be known among the Viennese as "the house without eyebrows" (for its lack of window frames) and was seen as an architectural anomaly. Supposedly, Emperor Franz Joseph, who lived across the street in the Hofburg Palace, nailed shut all the windows that overlooked Loos's signature building because he couldn't bear looking at the monstrosity.

Loos was a major influence on the Bauhaus in Germany and in France on Le Corbusier, who published *Ornament and Crime* in his magazine *L'Esprit Nouveau* in November 1920. Other important influences on the early Modernists came from nineteenth-century theories by German philosopher Friedrich Schlegel concerning the concept of "the interesting." In Schlegel's mind, the interesting did not necessarily follow conventional aesthetic principles, and its value existed exclusively because of its specialness. Interesting could be described as anything out of the norm, deviant, adventurous, disgusting, or even ugly. As a result, shock became a valid aesthetic strategy.

Form Follows Misunderstanding

–

Early in his career, Loos worked in the United States as a mason, a floor layer, and a dishwasher. He was fascinated by the efficiency of American architecture and admired the work of architect Louis Sullivan. It was Sullivan who coined the famous *form follows function* slogan in the late nineteenth century, which became the modernist rallying cry all throughout the twentieth century: "Whether it be the sweeping eagle in his flight, or the open apple-blossom, the toiling work-horse, the blithe swan, the branching oak, the winding stream at its base, the drifting clouds, over

all the coursing sun, form ever follows function, and this is the law."[10]

Sullivan's philosophy was inspired by architect Marcus Vitruvius Pollio, who believed every structure must be built with three goals: it must be solid, useful, and beautiful.

Sullivan himself, however, didn't always ascribe to his own directive—certainly not to the dogmatic extent to which it was adopted by the modernist movement. His widely admired entryway to the Carson Pirie Scott and Company Store in Chicago, for example, is richly decorated with undulating ironwork, featuring forms that neither follow nor provide any function.† The edict clearly resonated more deeply with Modernists than it did with its originator.

Many functionalists used Sullivan's maxim by claiming that when function is optimized, the form that follows will automatically be good. As we can easily experience when leaving any highway via an off-ramp—a ramp that works well, allowing for optimum traffic flow, and whose form follows its function perfectly—the overall formal result is not one most people would describe as good. Few people visit highway off-ramps on their holidays in order to spend time in a pleasing environment. While this example might feel rigged, as any highway construction is, by necessity, utilitarian, there are plenty of examples where function-driven infrastructure can also double as good space. The shack where the New York Department of Sanitation keeps its salt is just one example.

The New York Department of Sanitation stores its salt in this shed: a functional building that is also beautiful.

The End of Civilization: Beauty and World War I

—

Many artists returned from World War I psychologically scarred and disillusioned with the state of the world. Whereas prior to the war, beauty had been held as a moral value, after the war, the value of beauty's existence was called into question. If human beings could annihilate each other using industrial killing machines, what role, if any, should beauty play in our lives? Many believed it no longer had a role and needed to be eradicated from contemporary culture.

It's not surprising then that, in 1917, Marcel Duchamp tried to exhibit a ready-made urinal called *Fountain* as an anti-aesthetic statement. Some of his collectors defended the urinal,

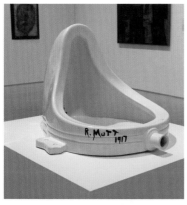

Marcel Duchamp's *Fountain*, 1917, an anti-aesthetic statement

Constantin Brâncuşi, *Head*, c. 1919–23

pointing to its curved lines as sensuous, in the vein of Constantin Brâncuşi. Duchamp defended the work as proof of his determination to eliminate beauty from art. He was no longer interested in what he called "retinal art," which was purely visual: "I thought to discourage aesthetics...I threw...the urinal into their faces as a challenge, and now they admire them for their aesthetic beauty."[11]

In 2004, *Fountain* was voted by five hundred museum directors, artists, curators, and collectors as the most important piece of art in the twentieth century.[12] The conceit of the ready-made has been embraced by the art world, influencing generations of artists since.

Corbu and the Destruction of Paris

—

The leading proponents of Modernism, Le Corbusier, Ludwig Mies van der Rohe, and Walter Gropius, emerged as the creators of a number of architectural masterpieces in Dessau, Germany, and elsewhere. The generation that followed misunderstood their ideas as some sort of economic functionalism that mandated the housing of as many people as efficiently possible. As a result, vast urban areas were overrun with giant building blocks of psychotic sameness that, in many cities, we still endure today.

Of course, Le Corbusier had some rather terrible ideas himself. He wanted to bulldoze large parts of Paris to make room for his own giant towers, separated by multi-lane highways. His proposal called for the separation of living and working areas, as well as a division between the rich and the poor. We now understand this as a display of abysmal stupidity. The living spaces would be deserted during the day and the work spaces dead at night. Traffic in between the two would be horrendous. City planners today recommend the exact opposite: mixed-use neighborhoods have far greater potential to be truly livable.

This is the work of Chicago architect Louis Sullivan, who coined the phrase

« *form follows function.* »
His own form follows no function. It just is.

Q:

*What's
the difference
between
God and
Le Corbusier?*

A:

God does not think he's Le Corbusier.

But then, of course, God is not a Modernist.[13]

Beauty and Modernism

—

We acknowledge the incredible beauty in the best of Modernism, and think many of Ellsworth Kelly's paintings are beautiful. We're great fans of Peter Zumthor's spa in Vals, Switzerland, which is one of the most magnificent interiors of the twentieth century; the tension between the rugged nature on the outside and the Zen-like interior creates a space in which even ten-year-old boys move around solemnly (without the need for a "quiet" sign).

Beauty in Modernism: Ellsworth Kelly

Beauty in Modernism: Peter Zumthor

Beauty in Modernism: Luis Barragán

We're also deeply impressed by Tadao Ando's museum complexes on Naoshima Island in Japan, where custom-built spaces were made to resonate with the art they house, creating a sense of both power and tranquility. And Mies van der Rohe's Seagram Building on Park Avenue in New York City fills us with awe when we enter that beautiful space.

The International Style: Economic Functionalism, Repetition, and Boredom

—

It seems that for every Seagram Building in Midtown Manhattan there are hundreds of structures like the Queensbridge housing project, just over the East River in Queens.

For every good modern building, there are hundreds of bad ones.

The original modernist embrace of functionality turned into pure economic functionalism by the 1950s. This economic functionalism not only was formally questionable but, ironically, did not do what its name promised: it did not function.

Housing projects did not work for housing humans because most people did not want to live there. Crime rates tended to increase around the projects, which caused vacancy rates to rise. Two or three decades later, many of these structures needed to be dynamited.

The Soviet Union developed factories that manufactured prefabricated housing systems that were built all over the Soviet empire and shipped to friendly nations throughout Europe, Asia, and South America.

Many housing projects were not effective for housing humans.

170 million apartments were hastily built across the globe.

During the second half of the twentieth century, more than 170 million hastily constructed apartments were installed worldwide. If we assume a family of three to four people lived in each one, this means more than half a billion people made their homes in these apartments. As the world population in 1975 was about four billion, every eighth person in the world lived in one of these blocky units![14]

And many of these people were busy exorcising Modernism out of their units by hanging little curtains, placing doilies and knickknacks everywhere, painting the interiors in bright colors, and fighting the original intent of the architecture as best as they could. Some experts are convinced that these

housing conditions were part of the reason communism ultimately fell.

Inhabitants of housing projects exorcising Modernism

While, in the past, different cultures developed their own architectural styles influenced by their local architectural heritage and their particular geography and climate, the International Style—a term coined in New York by Museum of Modern Art curators Henry-Russell Hitchcock and Philip Johnson to describe modernist architecture—supplanted this formal diversity with the universal box.

In the following decades, sameness became international and intentional. No matter what the climate or culture, everybody got a box. Roofs that were once steep to cope with heavy winter snowfalls were flattened, and required manual cleaning. Windows that were once limited and carefully positioned to take advantage of cool breezes during stifling summers were replaced with all-glass facades, necessitating artificial cooling. Regardless of whether you faced the freezing storms of Anchorage or the steaming heat of Dubai, whether your buildings were covered by sheets of ice or pelted by hot sandstorms, you received the same design solution.

Architecturally, the International Style proved most prevalent in Germany. With so many buildings destroyed during World War II, extensive rebuilding was desperately

An Austrian, a Swiss, and a German managed to convince the whole world how it should live.

They invented the International Style.

Adolf Loos

Le Corbusier

Mies van der Rohe

Bauhaus alumnus Fritz Ertl
created the

ultimate functionalist fuck you to humanity

by determining how to efficiently house as
many people as possible.

needed afterward. We'd assumed that the International Style was particularly successful in Germany because advocates of the style tended to lean left politically—a welcome break from the fascist ideology of the totalitarian Nazi regime. Yet Le Corbusier worked as an official city planner for the Vichy government in France, the people Hitler had put in charge during Germany's occupation. Mies van der Rohe participated in a competition to design the 1935 German Pavilion at the International Exposition in Brussels, and even his first sketch featured prominent swastika flags.[15] And Bauhaus alumnus Fritz Ertl created functionalism's final fuck you to humanity, the final solution to house people as efficiently as possible: the architecture of the barracks at the Auschwitz concentration camp.

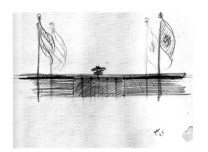

**Mies van der Rohe's sketch for
the German Pavilion**

And as already noted: the term *International Style* was coined within the newly formed architectural department at the Museum of Modern Art in New York, founded by the Nazi sympathizer Johnson.

Stick Figures in White Space
-

Rarely has the desire for functionality functioned more poorly than in this modernist Japanese Metro sign, which indicates that passengers should give up their seats for a pregnant woman.

The spare graphics of these signs made sense in the 1920s, when detailed color printing was

**Pregnant woman or person
with available Wi-Fi?**

expensive. Today, a carefully styled photograph of a pregnant woman would communicate more quickly and more effectively.

The German typographer Jan Tschichold was largely responsible for creating the modern page layout. He invented the idea of the page grid on which all visual elements were placed. He preferred a sans-serif typeface and asymmetrical compositions, all of which were outlined in his seminal book, *Die Neue Typographie*. His designs contained lots of carefully composed white space.

So Sorry, We Changed
Our Minds
-

But Tschichold later considered his views in *Die Neue Typographie* as too extreme and renounced Modernism in general as inherently authoritarian and fascist. He declared that sans-serif typefaces were simply not sufficiently legible and, therefore, unusable as body copy.

He discarded the modernist layout as early as 1932 and set type again in classic Roman typefaces. He was later responsible for overseeing the redesign of hundreds of Penguin paperbacks, all displaying classical typefaces such as Garamond, Janson, Baskerville, Bell, and Sabon, moving away from modernist sans-serif fonts.

JAN TSCHICHOLD

DIE NEUE TYPOGRAPHIE

EIN HANDBUCH FÜR ZEITGEMÄSS SCHAFFENDE

BERLIN **1928**
VERLAG DES BILDUNGSVERBANDES DER DEUTSCHEN BUCHDRUCKER

Jan Tschichold created the
modern page layout.

Nevertheless, the principles of his influential book are still taught in design schools around the world today. It seems that his strict rules and rigid grids just felt too comfortable for designers to give up. We still encounter many designers at conferences who talk about their love of white space and their fascination with the grid. No matter that it was developed in Germany almost a hundred years ago and was later renounced, this design strategy has remained the default style of corporate communication worldwide.

Another important Modernist with enormous influence on twentieth-century graphic design was the Swiss artist and designer Max Bill. In the 1950s, he stressed that beauty needed to play a more active role in design and that good work could not be achieved when the focus was solely on utility. In his important essay from 1949, "Beauty from Function and as Function," he stated, "It has become clear to us that beauty can no longer be developed out of function alone; instead, the demand for beauty has to be set on the same level as a functional demand, since it is a function, too."[16]

Kaboom! Kaboom! That was a dramatic departure from *form follows function,* which arguably became—alongside *less is more*—Modernism's most popular slogan.

Bill goes on to state, "We should no longer have to demand functionality, it ought to be a matter of course. The pursuit of beauty is much more difficult; it requires a greater effort."

Whenever a journalist brings up beauty in interviews with designers, the standard reaction is one of indignation: "Of course our work is not about making pretty things! We are problem solvers!" We suspect many of these designers do not know how to create beauty. We ourselves find that ideas are a dime a dozen, but executing a piece so that its form is beautiful as well as relevant to its time and culture is difficult.

Beauty is hard!

When hiring students and young designers for our studio, it's fairly easy to find candidates with strong concepts in their portfolios, but rarely do we see formally sophisticated work. Most design schools simply don't take it seriously, and their faculties—who were trained during the concept/utility-heavy second half of the twentieth century—often do not know how to teach it.

Pop Pops the Pop Art
—

Meanwhile, in the art world, Duchamp's ready-mades appeared in the midst of Cubism, Expressionism, and Futurism—all artistic movements where formal expression was central to the work. Futurism's famous manifesto stated, "We declare that the splendor of the world has been enriched with a new form of beauty, the beauty of speed.... A race-automobile...is more beautiful than the *Victory of Samothrace*."[17]

In the 1960s, Andy Warhol transitioned from working exclusively as a commercial artist to creating paintings, sculptures, and other works of fine art. It was Warhol who

Now Beijing looks like this

South Africa used to look like this

Now Munich looks like this

drove the effort to break down the barriers between the two creative genres. He explored new ways to challenge the dominant movement of the time—Abstract Expressionism, a field filled by formally obsessed macho types for whom he had little love. He declared that beauty was to be found only in the commercial: "The most beautiful thing in Tokyo is McDonald's. The most beautiful thing in Stockholm is McDonald's. The most beautiful thing in Florence is McDonald's. Peking and Moscow don't have anything beautiful yet."[18]

Warhol exhibited mock-ups of several different product boxes.

Only the Brillo box became a Pop art icon.

In an exhibit in 1964, Warhol showed mock-ups of several different commercial product boxes: Kellogg's Corn Flakes, DelMonte Peach Halves, Heinz Ketchup, Campbell's Tomato Juice, Mott's Apple Juice, and Brillo. It was the Brillo box that became his most famous sculpture and, eventually, a Pop art icon. This may well be connected to the fact that the Brillo box was originally designed by painter James

The Brillo box was designed by Abstract Expressionist painter James Harvey.

Harvey, the kind of artist Warhol was making fun of. Like most Abstract Expressionists of the time, Harvey had found it difficult to generate a steady income from his art and took on the odd commercial job; he created the design for the Brillo Manufacturing Company to make ends meet. So even when beauty was supposed to play no role—or only an ironically removed one—it found a way to sneak back into art history.

In contemporary art, *beauty* has become a dirty word. It is now situated somewhere below kitsch, which is accepted as an ironic stance. When we use kitsch, we can distance ourselves from beauty; we are allowed to keep our cynicism intact. No need to be sincere.

Personally we are very much in favor of *all* the strategies introduced into fine art during the twentieth century, *including* kitsch, shock, and disgust. But we do think that one hundred years after Duchamp introduced his urinal to the world, it is time to allow beauty back in.

The Here, Now, and Future of Beauty

Of course, gorgeous things can be found all over the World Wide Web, so it seems perplexing that the interfaces themselves are often designed within purely functionalist strategies, devoid of aesthetic consideration or visual appeal. Even companies such as Apple, whose products and packaging have clearly been designed with a high degree of sophistication (see the following chapter, "Experiencing Beauty"), seem to relegate their web presence to inferior designers. Apple's online efforts rarely deliver the same visual joy found in their products, packaging, and even advertising.

If we compare the mobile application designs of companies like Facebook, Airbnb, and Etsy, it seems their interfaces depend on the formal developments that originated in the 1920s. Too often, these interfaces seem interchangeable. We would think that a higher degree of visual diversity would work well for these brands, especially considering what vastly different businesses these three companies represent.

Austrian programmer Florian Hoenig suggests new parameters for a yet-to-be-founded field of computational aesthetics, the research for computational methods that can make aesthetic decisions similarly to humans. He discusses the problem of "aesthetic pollution" generated by much computer-aided design, arguing that both professionals and laypeople create an unprecedented amount of material, both on the web and offline, that promotes uniformity.[19] He is convinced that by building on the research of fields such as empirical aesthetics, psychology, and neuroscience, digital tools could be created to assist in the nurturing of beauty in the same way they now do with functional tasks. He suggests that this new field of study would concentrate on form rather than content.

There are indicators that the relationship between order and complexity will provide an excellent starting point for such research, as it has already been shown that certain measurable ratios are particularly pleasing to the human eye.

The mobile interfaces for Facebook, Airbnb, and Etsy: three very different companies look very similar.

1. Denis Dutton, "A Darwinian Theory of Beauty" (TED2010, Long Beach, CA, February 12, 2010); https://www.ted.com/talks/denis_dutton_a_darwinian_theory_of_beauty.

2. Ernst Mach, "On Symmetry," in Popular Scientific Lectures, trans. Thomas J. McCormack (Chicago: Open Court, 1895), 89–106.

3. Plato, "Philebus," in Complete Works, ed. John M. Cooper and D. S. Hutchinson (Indianapolis: Hackett, 1997), 454.

4. Konrad Paul Liessmann, Schoenheit (Vienna: Facultas Verlags und Buchhandels AG, 2009), 19.

5. Vitruvius, Ten Books on Architecture, trans. Ingrid D. Rowland (Cambridge: Cambridge University Press, 1999), bk. 1, 24–26.

6. Théophile Gautier, Mademoiselle de Maupin, trans. Helen Constantine (London: Penguin Classics, 2006), 22.

7. "There is but one way for the moderns to become great, and perhaps unequalled; I mean, by imitating the antients [sic]." Johann Joachim Winckelmann, Reflections on the Imitation of Greek Works in Painting and Sculpture, reprinted in The Art of Art History: A Critical Anthology, ed. Donald Preziosi (Oxford: Oxford University Press, 2009), 27.

8. Adolf Loos, Ornament and Crime (Riverside, CA: Ariadne, 1998), 168.

9. Loos, Ornament and Crime, 167.

10. Louis Sullivan, Kindergarten Chats and Other Writings (New York: Dover, 1979), 208. Although Sullivan's original words were "form ever follows function," the slogan has been condensed over the years and is now widely recognized as "form follows function."

11. Marcel Duchamp, quoted in Hans Richter, Dada: Art and Anti-Art (New York: McGraw Hill, 1965), 207-8.

12. Louise Jury, "'Fountain' Most Influential Piece of Modern Art," Independent, December 2, 2004, http://www.independent.co.uk/news/uk/this-britain/fountain-most-influential-piece-of-modern-art-673625.html.

13. We can state this with some confidence, as God wrote a book. In this book—the Bible—God outs himself as a designer of lighting fixtures. In Exodus 25:31, God gives Moses detailed manufacturing instructions: "And thou shalt make a candlestick of pure gold: of beaten work shall the candlestick be made: his shaft, and his branches, his bowls, his knops, and his flowers, shall be of the same."

14. Trent Fredrickson, "Chilean Pavilion Reflects upon Prefabricated Past at Venice Biennale," Designboom, June 11, 2014, https://www.designboom.com/architecture/chile-pavilion-prefabricated-past-venice-architecture-biennale-06-11-2014/.

15. Celina R. Welch, "Mies van der Rohe's Compromise with the Nazis," https://e-pub.uni-weimar.de/opus4/frontdoor/deliver/index/docId/1145/file/Celina_R_Welch.pdf.

16. Max Bill, "Beauty from Function and as Function," in Form, Function, Beauty = Gestalt, Architecture Words 5 (London: Architectural Association Publications, 2010), 34. See the German original: "Schönheit aus Funktion und als Funktion," Werk 36, no. 8 (1949): 272–74.

17. Filippo Tommaso Marinetti, The Foundation and Manifesto of Futurism, trans. Joshua C. Taylor, reprinted in Herschel B. Chipp, Theories of Modern Art: A Source Book for Artists and Critics (Berkeley and Los Angeles: University of California Press, 1968), 286.

18. Andy Warhol, The Philosophy of Andy Warhol: From A to B and Back Again (New York: Houghton Mifflin Harcourt, 2014), 71.

19. Florian Hoenig, "Defining Computational Aesthetics," in Proceedings of the First Eurographics Conference on Computational Aesthetics in Graphics, Visualization and Imaging (Girona, Spain: Eurographics Association, 2005), 13–18.

Pt. —

Experien

F ew important artists working today talk openly about beauty as a goal for their art. It is possible to create a career based on kitsch—garish beauty and sentimentality as ironic statements—as Jeff Koons has so consistently proven. But the sincere and unequivocal pursuit of beauty has been largely exiled from the contemporary art world.*

Jeff Koons, *Michael Jackson and Bubbles*, **1988**

Of course, there are contemporary artists who create beautiful work. We suspect that members of this relatively small group would rather not talk about beauty publicly for fear of being labeled old-fashioned or reactionary. One can still claim the mantle of the avant-garde by presenting ready-mades in the twenty-first century, even though this more than century-old concept has been recycled hundreds of times. In our view, taking a found object and declaring it art in 2018 is a singularly boring strategy.

The American artist Chuck Close railed against the term *de-skilled* art in a *New York Times Magazine* story while praising the pursuit of form and arguing for a studio practice that focuses on skill and technique, not just concept. After he became paralyzed in 1988, he thought: "I can make work of a conceptual nature. I can put a level on a shelf as well as someone else! But I was going to miss the activity of pushing paint around."[1] In the latter part of his career, with a well-established following, Close can afford to ignore the current fashions and opinions influencing the art market.

When we talk about beauty, we really mean formal intent. By working to create a beautiful design or object, we're committing ourselves to a higher standard. With the appropriate training, any designer can craft an object that functions. We assume function and seek higher ground. The final result of a designer's well-considered efforts might, in fact, be ugly. Regardless, we applaud the effort and appreciate the pursuit of a considered formal goal.

Design, with its inherently commercial agenda, rarely risks alienating—at least intentionally—potential consumers. Fine art, on the other hand, sometimes cultivates, intentionally or not, negative reactions. One can look at Damien Hirst's *Black Sun* painting and see incredible beauty, although we assume he created it in the spirit of provocation, aiming to disgust viewers.

Damien Hirst, *Black Sun*, **2004**

Seen from afar, Hirst's work could double as one of Richard Serra's paint-stick drawings: a rich, black circle against a white wall. As we move closer to the work, we discover that the deep black is made up of thousands of dead flies, creating significant tension between the Zen-like minimalism and the sheer multitude of insect corpses.

Surely the strategy of shocking or disgusting the bourgeoisie has run its course within the contemporary art world. It's become difficult to create anything offensive. Many years have passed since viewers could be shocked by an image of a highly abstracted naked woman descending a staircase.[*] An artist's shit packed into a can is old news now.[†]

When the Viennese art collective Gelitin exhibited in the Kunsthaus Bregenz in the conservative Austrian county of Vorarlberg, it thought of its efforts as shock's last hurrah. (Most likely, the same exhibit would not have found a space in New York City, where audiences are rarely offended.) Gelitin showed a video of hard-boiled eggs being shoved up the anus of a man; he then mimicked the Easter Bunny by defecating the eggs. Gelitin's strategy was successful: letters to the editor of the *Vorarlberger Nachrichten* demanded the dismissal of the museum's director.

Austrian collective Gelitin at the Kunsthaus Bregenz

The American artist James Turrell travels an entirely different path. He is the rare contemporary artist who unapologetically pursues beauty in his work. His recent—and possibly largest—"skyspace," installed at Rice University in Houston, Texas, encourages viewers to see the arrival of dusk (or dawn) through a square opening in the ceiling. Viewed in the evening, the sky transforms from a familiar sky blue to a dark blue, and then deepens to an extra dark blue, never quite turning black, producing the darkest of dark blues—a blue so dark that it isn't printable or paintable. It's the darkest blue imaginable because it's made by the universe! There is a deep beauty in that, a beauty that has meaning.

Icelandic-born artist Ragnar Kjartansson created the exhibition *Me, My Mother, My Father, and I* at the New Museum in New York City in 2014. In the show, he projected a video featuring his parents—now both established figures in the opera and music worlds—in their youth, performing in a soft-porn film, presumably to finance their studies. Kjartansson translated the words from the film and had musicians sing these lyrics in a song composed by Sigur Rós: "Take me by the dishwasher, yes, I'm getting desperate...."

The song played nonstop, from when the museum opened in the morning until closing time in the evening. The combination of gorgeous melodies, silly lyrics, and the obvious dedication of the musicians created an experience that can only be described as sublime. Kjartansson took these disparate elements and through endless repetition was able to create a transcendent mantra.

Is There Gorgeousness in Modernism?
—

There are many wonderful examples of architectural Modernism where beauty was intended and realized.

During Stefan's sabbatical in Mexico, he visited a number of Luis Barragán's houses. Barragán is commonly acknowledged as a master of Mexican Modernism. While some of the actual buildings don't live up to the famous photos, the Casa Pedregal, owned by César Cervantes, is impressive in its exalted beauty. In this work, Barragán combined an undulating, lava-based exterior with a structured interior to create a mesmerizing whole. Unlike their German counterparts, a number of Latin American Modernists were aware of the power of contrast, pairing straight lines with curving natural elements. A clean structure tends to work much better when it's situated amid lush topography rather than in the boring flatlands of the former East Germany.

Casa Pedregal encompasses more than one thousand square meters of interior space

† In 1961 Italian artist Piero Manzoni created ninety cans of Artist's Shit, each numbered 001–090.

* Marcel Duchamp's Nude Descending a Staircase No. 2 stirred an uproar when it debuted in 1912.

with a configuration so carefully arranged you get the sense of swimming through an abstract narrative. Like a three-dimensional Piet Mondrian painting, the space is perfectly composed from every vantage point. While the effect is certainly extraordinary, it still feels like a home, as opposed to a museum or stage set. César recalled that Barragán was reluctant to take on the commission but finally agreed, with three stipulations: First, the client would not be allowed to enter the building site until the house was completed.[*] Second, Barragán would select all furnishings and artwork. Third, there would be no budget.

The late, great Oscar Niemeyer designed many buildings in Brazil. In a video interview, he recalls a visit from Walter Gropius, founder of the Bauhaus, to his private home in the mountains overlooking Rio de Janeiro—he had spent years searching for the perfect site. He recounts Gropius asking him if the house were replicable, after which Niemeyer looked into the camera, slapped his knees, and proclaimed Gropius "an idiot!"[2]

We doubt that the words *Gropius* and *idiot* have ever been uttered in the same sentence in Germany.

Waves in the Harbor
-

It is immediately apparent that creating a beautiful design was on the minds of the Swiss architects Jacques Herzog and Pierre de Meuron when they built the Elbphilharmonie concert hall in Hamburg, Germany, in 2017. We visited the building during construction and the still-raw spaces made evident that the architects took advantage of many brand-new technologies; for instance, the large auditorium rests on springs and is decoupled from the rest of the building for acoustic reasons. The undulating forms of this spectacular crystal palace would not have been possible twenty years earlier.

The building is the new symbol for Hamburg. Situated in a prime harbor location where two canals meet, it is built on top of a historic warehouse. The edifice, with its ever-changing appearance according to time of day and vantage point, is an unmitigated success.

Herzog & de Meuron's Elbphilharmonie, VitraHaus, and Allianz Arena: three projects, three strategies

When Frank Gehry built his emblematic Guggenheim Museum Bilbao, he put the Spanish industrial city on the map for international travelers, as well as art and architecture enthusiasts. Hence the term *the Bilbao effect*, which led numerous cities to follow suit and commission Gehry to design shiny, titanium-skinned buildings in the hope of drawing visitors. For

* Luis Barragán built and tore down many walls when he did not get it quite right.

many cities, however, the Bilbao effect did not work. Herzog & de Meuron's strategy—to innovate site-specifically and create new strategies and forms for every project—has proven considerably more successful.

Of course, the most significant direct predecessor of the Elbphilharmonie is the Sydney Opera House, perhaps the most recognizable building of the twentieth century. Its functions far exceed the successful performance space for singers, orchestras, and audiences. It combines ancient and archetypal architectural forms with modernist ideas, resulting in a new and singular symbol of Australia.

The Triumph of the iPhone
-

At conferences, lots of people we encounter tend to pontificate about some lesson learned using Apple as a case study supporting their arguments. It can get boring. So, it's with some trepidation that we look at Apple's history to reinforce our beliefs about creating beauty. Beauty was on Steve Jobs's mind all his life, and he clearly subscribed to the idea that beauty is as important as functionality when developing insanely great products. As journalist Pascal-Emmanuel Gobry wrote, "After all, it wouldn't be unfair to say that Steve Jobs's entire career can be summed up as the stubborn insistence that the stuff of everyday life, the stuff that surrounds us, shouldn't just be efficient or useful, but also must be beautiful. And countless millions of people have voted their assent to this with their cold, hard cash."[3]

There is no smartphone today that does not take its cues from the iPhone, the most influential design artifact of the last decade. Its success can be attributed to thousands of decisions, many of them informed by aesthetics.

When Stefan spoke with Apple's Chief Design Officer Jonathan Ive at a conference at the Art Center in California, Ive recalled the making of the iMac stand.[*] At the time Apple's Chinese manufacturer thought it impossible to create the stand as a single piece and suggested a two-part approach, which would require a thin seam. This seam would be hidden behind the screen and remain invisible to most users. Ive thought the seam unattractive and pressed the manufacturer, who simply refused to accommodate him. So Ive suggested that Apple search for a new manufacturer.

One would need to care immensely about the physical appearance of the product in order to agree to Ive's suggestion. For the CEO of a publicly held computer company, the pressures of creating a new product are extraordinary, the competition is fierce, and the race to bring the innovations to market as fast as possible is intense. In this context, Ive wanted Apple to find and hire a new Chinese manufacturer because he didn't like the look of a seam at the back of the machine. Millions of computers would be made, and new questions about reliability and quality control would inevitably crop up. These questions would all need to be resolved quickly and with an unfamiliar partner. Ultimately, Jobs agreed with Ive. Apple changed manufacturers, and the iMac was shipped without a seam.

Apple is one of the only giant consumer-product companies that properly understands the theatrical nature of unwrapping. Taking a cue from centuries of Japanese packaging design, the Apple design team considers every layer that will need to be peeled away with love, care, and full attention. Of course, the main function of the packaging is to ensure that the product arrives safely. But the Apple designers did manage to add another essential function to the process: joy.

Form Replaces Function
-

Philippe Starck's Juicy Salif lemon squeezer became a symbol of the design boom of the

* Jonathan Ive was principal designer for the iMac, iPod, and iPhone.

1990s and, in the eyes of many, gave design a bad name. It was accused of not working very well (it works fine, but does make a little mess) and for being overly expensive.

A lemon press can have numerous functions. Yes, certainly critical is its ability to press lemons. But in addition, it can function as a way of displaying taste and status, it can tell us something about the times we live in, and it can be a conversation starter—even if that conversation is about the function (or lack thereof) of the press itself.

Essentially, Starck designed a small sculpture for the kitchen, a space formerly devoid of artistic objects. He took the lemon squeezer out of the utensil drawer and placed it on the kitchen counter. He also gave it a contemporary form appropriate for our time. Seen as a sculpture, the piece can be considered affordable: an opportunity to own a work of art. And if one of the functions of the design of any object is to be economical (i.e., to be able to advertise and sell itself), Starck's press fulfilled that extraordinarily well: Alessi sold ten thousand of its later-issued, gold-plated version alone.

Our friend the Dutch designer Hella Jongerius famously asked, "Who'd want to ruin a perfectly good vase by putting flowers in it?"[4]

But before you react in horror to such self-indulgence, it might be worth mentioning that the strategy to create high-end utilitarian objects that were never meant to be used was not invented by ego-driven designers at the end of the twentieth century—it actually has significant historic precedence. During a visit to the Munich Residenz, we were told that the porcelain dining set commissioned by the German emperor was never, ever in use and was put on display immediately after it was created.

If we push the design of a chair to such an extent that you cannot sit on it anymore, it becomes a sculpture. We can then decide if it's a good sculpture or not.

Marc Newson designed a bookshelf in 2007 out of a single piece of Carrara marble.[*] It sold in an edition of eight at a price tag of $1 million each. From a functional point of view, the shelf works no better than a couple of Billy shelves, available at IKEA. From a beauty point of view—meaning a combination of form, color, material, and surface that pleases our aesthetic senses—the two are in different galaxies.

The Final Holdout: Fashion
—

Arguably the only area of the applied arts where beauty never went away and remained an important goal for designers throughout the twentieth century is fashion.[†] From Coco Chanel to Christian Dior, Yves Saint Laurent to Iris van Herpen, top fashion designers have considered beauty critically important to everything they created. This included their couture and ready-to-wear lines, and extended to the packaging of their perfumes and the production of their runway shows. This was never displayed more memorably than at our favorite fashion exhibit of all time, the excellent *Manus x Machina* at the Metropolitan Museum of Art in New York in 2016. Although the main strategy of the show was to compare the handmade to the machine-made, every single one of the more than 170 pieces on view served as an argument for the importance of beauty in everyday life. We might be willing to compromise when it comes to the cities we live in or the architecture we inhabit, but when the objects are worn close to the skin, many of us demand they be created with strong formal intent. While numerous functionalists tried to influence fashion, women often simply refused to wear their gray smocks.

The International Style's influence on fashion design is, of course, apparent today in the work of high-end designers like Jil Sander and Raf Simons, but some consumers reject the style's ideas. While many agree to live within modernist city planning and in modernist

[†] And, of course, there's jewelry: all form, no function.

[*] Marc Newson was also involved in the design of the Apple Watch.

Our friend the Dutch designer Hella Jongerius
famously asked,

« Who'd want to ruin a perfectly good vase by putting flowers in it? »

Fashion and Modernism

architecture, the human desire for individuality, self-expression, and adornment in what they wear mostly does win out.

This might also be a reason why fashion Instagram feeds are so popular. Fashion designers such as Stefano Ricci and Stefano Gabbana have millions of followers on this inherently visual platform, while architects and product designers are lagging behind.

Instagram and the Tyranny of the Good-Looking (Life)

—

Among the large social media platforms, Instagram is most closely associated with aesthetics. (Facebook's focus is social connection; Snapchat is too short-lived for people to bother about form.) Not everything "liked" on Instagram is necessarily beautiful (or even trying to be)—there are plenty of successful streams filled with images of wacky dogs and cat videos. Regardless, Instagram is a visually driven site.

We don't see Instagram as a purely positive force. It is a highly curated view of our lives, and instead of being a way of sharing our days with people we like, it has emerged as a tool for showing an idealized view of reality. It generates as much envy as pleasure.

Although the negative aspects of Instagram have been scrutinized tirelessly, Jessica believes the positive aspects of the platform have been somewhat overlooked. Access to a seemingly infinite range of imagery has brought an understanding of beauty to a much wider audience. Friends and family outside the creative world have told Jessica that Instagram has helped them develop a better eye, or appreciate design more, or learn about work they never knew existed. Through Instagram, she has discovered beautiful places to visit, and found artists and designers making beautiful things with whom we can collaborate, as well as commission.

She points to the intrinsic democratization that is inherent in the Instagram platform. Instead of relying on a few judges or editors or curators at the top making decisions about what should or should not be seen—as at magazines or museums or galleries—it gives anyone a chance to find recognition. If you post beautiful things, no matter how small your following, you could be featured in Instagram's Find gallery (Instagram has a complex algorithm that determines when users find something interesting, regardless of how small their following). Once in that gallery, you'll be picked up by other sources and reposted, and can gain additional followers quickly. Jessica knows many people who attribute their entire careers to Instagram and say it has given them the freedom to live wherever they want in the world and continue to engage with the community they have built. You no longer need to know the right people or live in the right city to find success.

In addition, anyone can become a curator now, if you have the urge. Jessica curates creative works on Instagram, and these works often enjoy a larger audience than they would if exhibited in most design museums. The

Opposite page: A 3-D printed dress by New York design collective threeASFOUR

artists and designers she posts regularly report they've been commissioned and/or have increased sales after she shares their work.

We've also found the dialogues and communities on Instagram to be quite positive and supportive compared to other social media platforms, which is interesting given that it's a more beauty-driven medium. On the opposite end of the spectrum is Twitter. As a text-driven platform, it performs a very simple function: to communicate messages to a broad audience in 280 (originally, 140) characters or less. It has become the go-to forum for complaining and trash-talking.

Communicating Beautifully
—

Looking through the "about" sections on the websites of graphic, communication, and motion design companies, they claim to be *interdisciplinary*, they talk about the importance of *storytelling*, they assert that they *create experiences*. Nobody mentions beauty. We don't know of a single important design company that includes beauty as a goal in its mission statement.

In communication design, beauty got a bad name through superficial beautification (i.e., taking something inferior and making it appear to be of better quality). One of the main reasons we buy a certain expensive shower gel is its superior aesthetics—we simply don't want an ugly one visually polluting our shower shelves every morning. We find ourselves forced to hide laundry detergent and window cleaning sprays in closets so they won't insult our eyes every time we come across them. There are perfectly fine products that come in packaging designed with few aesthetic goals; we just don't want to have to look at them.

When we realized that beauty improved the functionality of any project we designed, it began to play a larger role within our own work. The city of Amsterdam asked us to invigorate a newly built residential plaza. The production budget for this project was 6,000 euros, so we went to the Central Bank in Amsterdam and exchanged the 6,000 euros for 600,000 single euro cent coins.

The bank gave us old, dark coins; medium-colored ones; and brand-new, shiny coins. With the help of one hundred volunteers, we laid them out over the course of a week, using the existing stone tiles as our guiding grid, and spelling out the sentence *Obsessions make my life worse and my work better*. We tried to make the type as pretty as possible.

The city of Amsterdam asked us to invigorate a newly built residential plaza.

The piece would be left unguarded; we wanted to force the viewers to ask themselves, "Do I want to keep the beauty of the piece intact, or do I want to take the money?" We painted the backsides of the coins a particular shade of blue so that we could track their distribution all over Europe through a custom-built website.

The neighbors living around this plaza who'd watched us placing the coins on the stone tiles fell in love with the piece. On opening day, a visitor came with a big plastic bag and, as we'd anticipated, took as much money as he could carry. One of the neighbors called the police. When the police arrived, they reasoned, "This is art, so we need to protect it. Let's sweep it all up and take it to police headquarters for safekeeping."

The design lasted only a couple of hours. There was no need for any coin tracking.[5]

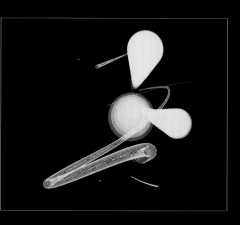

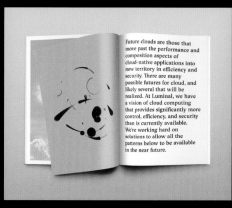

Future clouds are those that move past the performance and composition aspects of cloud-native applications into new territory in efficiency and security. There are many possible futures for cloud, and likely several that will be realized. At Luminal, we have a vision of cloud computing that provides significantly more control, efficiency, and security than is currently available. We're working hard on solutions to allow all the patterns below to be available in the near future.

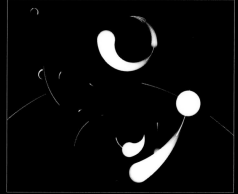

Obsessions Make My Life Worse and My Work Better (detail)

The Power of the Purely Aesthetic

—

We were hired to create a brand identity for Fugue, a company that develops software to help large corporations place giant amounts of data in the cloud. The software replaces itself with a new version several times per second, rendering scheduled updates unnecessary. The need for maintenance is replaced with automated regeneration.

We decided to bring an aesthetic-driven strategy to this project with one of our regular commercial clients. It was clear that ephemerality, as well as regeneration, was deeply rooted in the company's DNA, and we wanted to bring these concepts to the forefront in the visual language used for the identity itself. We purposefully avoided the clichés of the world of cloud software security systems—safes, padlocks, prison bars, etc.—and opted for a more conceptual approach, less focused on familiar metaphors.

Fugue's main marketing opportunities take place within specialized trade shows, attended by chief technology officers of large companies. When Fugue launched its new branding, its comparatively small booth was mobbed by international technology executives, and its T-shirts and tote bags were the most popular at the show. Beauty functioned (see p. 95).

This brand identity was also reviewed favorably on design websites, although a number of our fellow designers considered it too

self-indulgent, too pretty. Typical comments read: "Yes, this is nice, but beautiful graphics are not going to propel the business forward." This criticism became so pervasive that the CEO of Fugue felt compelled to comment, explaining that we designed it this way because we believed it would function better than if it had been created with the typical *designed to be functional* strategy.

Up in the Air

—

Airlines claim that safety is their absolute priority. They have all adopted the most efficient way to inform passengers about the locations of emergency exits and procedures: laminated cards with graphic icons derived directly from Otto Neurath's Isotype system, designed during the very beginnings of Modernism.

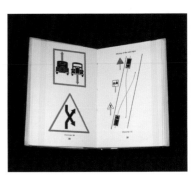

Otto Neurath's Isotype system was hugely influential on the design of instructional communications.

Since we both fly a lot, we've compiled a collection of hundreds of these cards over the years.* And during all these flights, we've never, ever noticed a passenger taking the card out of the seat back pocket to study it.

This means the cards serve no function. Their communication value is zero.

When Virgin rethought the entire strategy, travelers finally took notice. Instead of the usual cards, the designers at Virgin took advantage of the small TV screens already installed in front of each seat and created an

* Yes, we did notice the "do not remove from plane" warning printed on many of them.

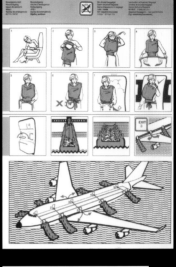

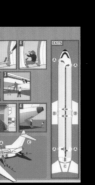

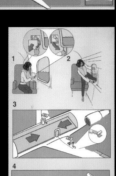

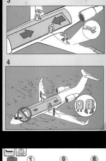

These icons work well enough in theory to get the go-ahead during the approval process in a corporate meeting. In the everyday life of international air travel, however, they do not work well at all. Passengers simply ignore them.

Airlines realized there was a problem and printed the emergency card on the back of the tray table to force passengers to look at it.

entertaining musical communicating the exact same content.

This emergency exit musical has received more than twelve million views on YouTube. Virgin has reached people who haven't even flown (or at least not recently) on its airline! This is proper functionalism. Other airlines have followed suit and produced their own versions of a tongue-in-cheek emergency video, but few are as entertaining as the original.

The safety video from Virgin America: no seat belt left unbuckled

Our Very Own Modernism
—

Sadly, we are guilty, too. When the subject veered toward contemporary architecture, as in a book we designed for the Columbia University Graduate School of Architecture, we stupidly reverted to a classic modernist layout, complete with grid-based body copy, lots of white space, and sans-serif typography. This layout says: Do not read me. I will bore the living shit out of you.

Later on, we discovered a couple of typos in the text. But it did not matter, as nobody had noticed because nobody had ever read the text.[*] Which means that the text actually functions as an ornament. But it's not even an honest ornament signaling "I'm here to be pretty," but a pretentious ornament, an ornament giving you the illusion of substance.

It pretends to inform but does not.

This layout says, "Do not read me."

Beauty as a Shortcut to Make Decisions Fast
—

As already mentioned, Dr. Helmut Leder, head of the Institute for Empirical Aesthetics in Vienna, suspects that beauty can be seen as a shortcut for the brain. For the brain to actually think takes lots of energy, so it wants to preserve this energy by using a shortcut to make fast decisions. The most beautiful wins.[†]

If Leder's hypothesis is correct, it would make sense for every packaging design company in the world to include beauty as a stated goal for its designs. But we don't know of a single packaging design studio that speaks with its clients about the value of beauty in design (except for perhaps the fashion and beauty industries).

In most supermarkets, the choices are between one functionally designed orange-juice box and many others like it. Most of these cartons communicate some version of *juicy* and *fresh* but not necessarily in a beautiful way or with a beautiful result. Most reasonable

WHICH OF THESE DETERGENT PACKAGES DO YOU THINK IS THE MOST BEAUTIFUL?

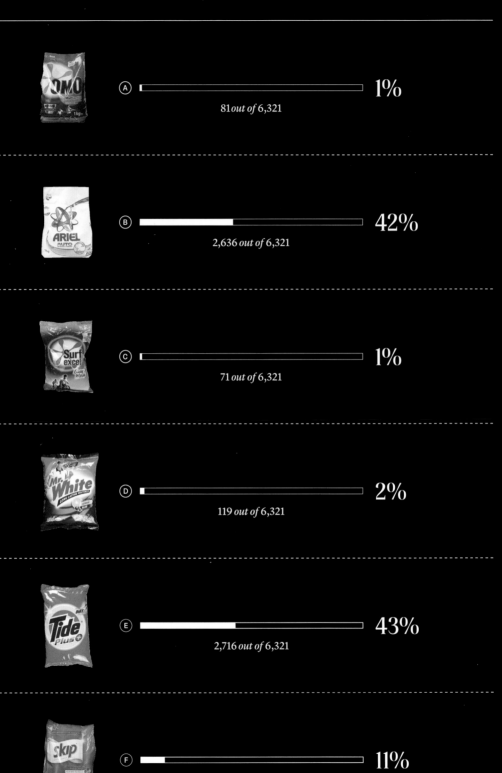

(A)   1%
81 out of 6,321

(B)   42%
2,636 out of 6,321

(C)   1%
71 out of 6,321

(D)   2%
119 out of 6,321

(E)   43%
2,716 out of 6,321

(F)   11%
698 out of 6,321

people would describe the visual world of our supermarkets as distinctly not beautiful. Our American supermarket shelves are filled with ugly packaging. (Although it doesn't have to be this way. In Japan, almost everything in the supermarkets looks attractive.)

When a client asks us, "Why have you designed it this way?" the answer is often, "Because it's more beautiful." It will function better (i.e., sell more units) if it is more beautiful. Creating beauty should be in the interest of any brand trying to take advantage of the brain's shortcut.

We asked our Instagram followers which of six detergent packages they found most beautiful.[6] The results were clear, with the winner getting forty times (!) as many votes as the package that came in last.

Tide and Ariel were the winners by a wide margin. If we were chief marketing officers of Omo or Surf Excel, we would do something about that.

There are also distinct preferences within a single brand and product, as our next survey, on Coca-Cola, shows (see pp. 111–12).[7] There were multiple redesign efforts on the classic can. The design team at Coca-Cola should be celebrating, as all its most recent designs are outperforming the previous ones. For once, a redesign actually did improve the package.

We recently did a rebrand for one of the largest US beverage companies. It was refreshing in its nostalgic but modern style of illustration, and everyone we tested the new packaging and branding on responded positively. The design team at the company loved it, but toward the end of the process a new chief marketing officer was appointed—and he killed our proposal. He wanted to clutter the package design with redundant information and "refreshment cues" (i.e., bubbles showing smiling people, demonstrating that this product will make you happy; text that literally says, "It's refreshing"). We need to move beyond these tedious paradigms.

We surveyed six other prominent brands—some went through recent and extensive redesigns—and asked our followers which they found to be most beautiful (see pp. 113–14).[8]

Of course, beauty is certainly not the only function when determining the success of a logo. One would think in the case of the Metropolitan Museum of Art, with its world-class collection of beautiful works, though, that beauty would play a prominent role in its visual identity. Coming in way after a credit card provider and a coffee chain, sandwiched between a computer manufacturer and a package shipper, could be seen as a somewhat disappointing result for America's most visited art museum.

In contrast, we have a client in India, Parle Agro, that recognizes the value of beautiful design and was willing to take a risk to do something different. The campaigns and rebrands we designed for the company have met with huge success. Frooti, its mango juice, saw a 60 percent increase in sales after our rebrand. We hope that someday corporations will take their cues from what scientists suspect and what we designers know to be true: beauty works!

Japanese packaging delivers a subtle piece of unwrapping theater.

Japan has known this for thousands of years. From low-end convenience stores like 7-Eleven to high-end *wagashi* shops that sell traditional Japanese sweets in Tokyo's Ginza district, beauty is everywhere. Stefan is confident that the attractive packaging not only convinced him to buy lots of Japanese sweets but that being around beauty constantly made a positive impact on his mood during his time there. The incredible love and attention that goes into Japanese packaging does not come across as wasteful or boastful, but rather delivers a subtle piece of unwrapping theater.

But elaborate packaging is tough to pull off. When Stefan served as a judge for an Asian design competition, he was overwhelmed by hundreds of Chinese moon cake packages. Most of them featured shiny gold typography on elaborately embossed red backgrounds, complete with hot-stamped dragon illustrations, which require the removal of multiple layers of transparent paper until one finally reaches the cakes themselves. The effect is unsatisfying—a simple, sweet treat trapped inside an inefficient, overproduced package.

A consumer packaging system with much less of a waste problem—that is, it does not get thrown out—is the vinyl album cover. Holding a special place within the world of packaging design, it remains in people's homes along with their music. Many covers have become iconic, and fans can easily conjure up an image in their minds when they hear the words *Sgt. Pepper's* or *Dark Side of the Moon*. Designers love the medium, as it offers the opportunity to visualize highly emotional but inherently nonvisual content—the music— with few design restrictions or limitations.[*]

The art of the album cover started with Alex Steinweiss in the 1930s and '40s and reached its zenith in the '70s and '80s, when the work of the British studio Hipgnosis dominated the scene. By the '90s, the CD cover reduced the available space to a five-by-five-inch square. Although the format offered better storytelling possibilities through sometimes elaborate booklets, the majority of CDs came packed in low-quality plastic jewel cases, which considerably reduced the consumer's satisfaction.

During the '90s, the studio designed many CD covers for bands you've never heard of, but also for some familiar bands, such as the Rolling Stones, the Talking Heads, and Lou Reed.[9] We left the world of music packaging around the year 2000, just before the near collapse of the music industry. As executives at the labels were anxious about their jobs—the industry's sales and distribution model was being challenged by online sharing platforms—very little innovative work was created during the first decade of the new millennium.

To our great surprise, the art of the album cover is in the midst of a renaissance. The work produced over the last couple of years by small, independent (often musician-owned) labels exceeds the quality of cover art from almost any previous period. We're often blown away by the newly released and carefully executed graphic experiments displayed on the shelves of Brooklyn's giant vinyl store Rough Trade. Without listening to the music in the store, we find ourselves selecting albums by the quality of their covers and have found that many great covers actually contain great music, allowing a whole new sonic world to reveal itself.

Most other shoppers in the store are in their twenties and weren't alive during the original heyday of vinyl. They download music through the accompanying links provided within the packaging and leave the vinyl record itself in mint condition. Stefan installed shelves at home to allow for the simultaneous display of four different covers. As the music changes, he adjusts the artwork, which allows him to see a fresh composition on the wall every few days. Although he owns some beautiful prints by Donald Judd and John Baldessari, these two skinny shelves hold the "best art I own." Given that a vinyl album sells for about $25, the $100 invested in four is a small fraction of what you'd pay for anything in the galleries of Chelsea. In terms of pure creativity and formal quality, the best of the current album covers compare well with the art world's offerings.

[*] In comparison, the film poster offers fewer rewards, since it basically compresses the visual content of the film into a single image.

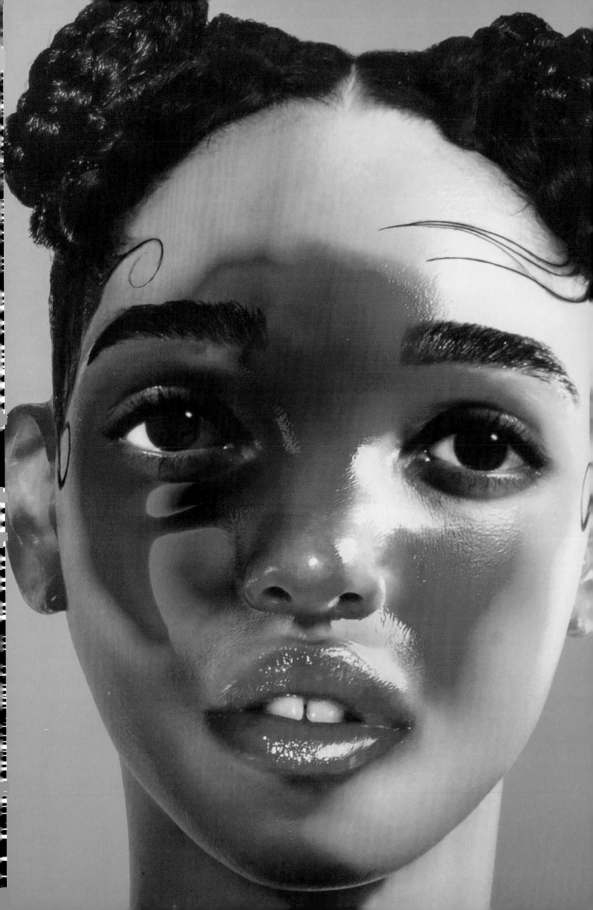

The Other Senses

—

When the studio was involved in music packaging, we were often jealous of the work of our clients. Beauty is rooted in music and can evoke a deep emotional response. Stefan's mood can be altered by shutting off the lights, sitting on the sofa, and listening to Darkside, Glass Animals, or our client Pat Metheny. He fears the covers the studio designed for Metheny, sadly, don't have the same transformational power.

Our cover for Pat Metheny's *Imaginary Day* did not deliver the same transformational power as his music.

Beginning in the twentieth century, a strain of classical music emulated the visual arts and rejected beauty in favor of more dissonant strategies. Some composers preferred difficult and sometimes jarring passages over straightforward melodies. Much of this music has failed to attract the audience that routinely flocks to galleries, fairs, and museums. While there are many people clearly interested in contemplating visual pieces they may or may not understand, far fewer seem willing to sit through a two-hour concert they might find challenging. It's OK when I can stroll by it, but it's not OK when I'm stuck in a room with it.

As stated earlier, familiarity plays a prominent role in the perception of beauty. The most successful stadium tours in the world are ones featuring bands such as U2 and Pink Floyd, who regularly play their most popular songs. At the beginning of any tour, the Rolling Stones play a maximum of two new songs sprinkled into their offerings of hits from the last five decades. The LCD Soundsystem documentary on the band's supposed final tour and concert was aptly titled *Shut Up and Play the Hits*.

A Beautiful Smell

—

Stefan had a crush on a woman for a number of years. She was in a relationship, so nothing came of it. When that relationship ended and they finally got together, he discovered she smelled like his sister, and the infatuation went out the window. As the German expression goes, "Ich kann dich nicht riechen" ("I cannot smell you"). The nose governs attractions and behaviors.

Within the fine and applied arts, smell is the least applied of all the senses. While the commercial perfume industry flourishes, exhibitions about or even just including smell are rare. Architects Elizabeth Diller, Ricardo Scofidio, and Charles Renfro created *The Art of Scent* at the Museum of Arts and Design in New York City, and the Norwegian artist Sissel Tolaas is rather active in considering the particularities of the nose in her work. Minor attempts at addressing the olfactory have been made in films, such as John Waters's *Polyester*, for which scratch-and-sniff Odorama cards were given to audience members to activate during the film. But these examples are few and far between.

Similar to the visual world, there is wide agreement across vast geographic areas and cultures on what we consider a good smell.

Israeli neurobiologist Rafi Haddad and his colleagues worked with a digital eNose device to rank various smells by their pleasantness and beauty.[10] They tested a range of smells on people from two different cultures: Israeli and Ethiopian. They discovered a consensus in smell preference, noting that people judged

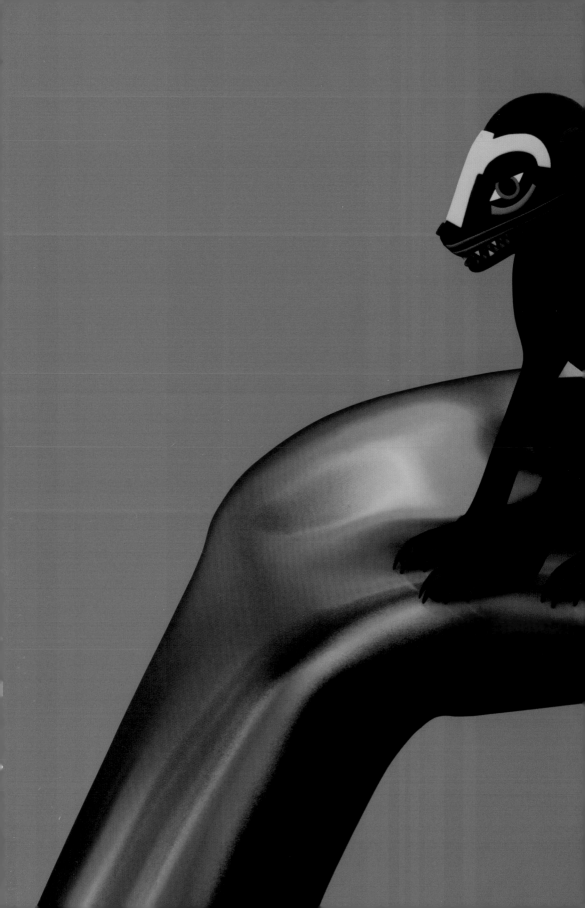

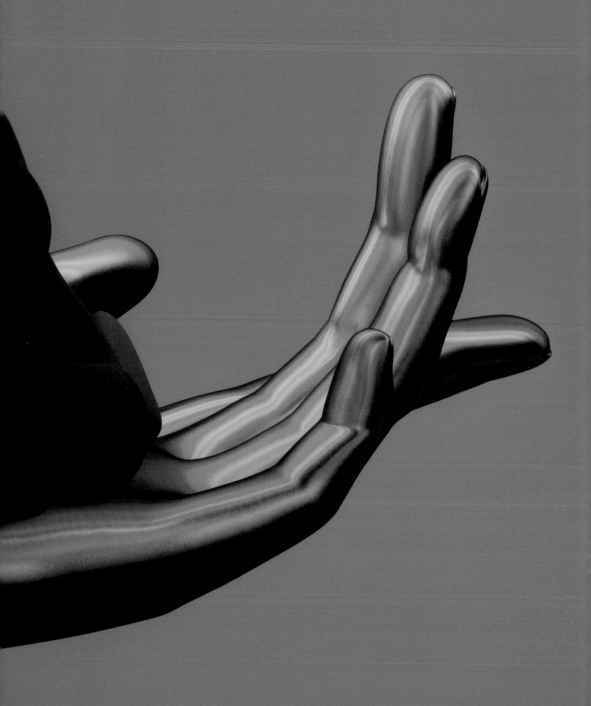

SBTRKT, *Wonder Where We Land* (2014)

the same smells as pleasant or not. It seems smells are biologically hardwired.

The following scents came in as winners:

1. lime
2. grapefruit
3. bergamot
4. orange
5. peppermint

When the *Daily Mail* surveyed its readers for their favorite smells, just-baked bread came in on top, closely followed by bacon, freshly cut grass, coffee, and vanilla. The worst smells included sewage and vomit.[11]

There are currently more than one thousand women's perfumes on sale in the United States alone.* If we look at the best-selling sector within this $8 billion industry, floral smells come in on top. While citrus-based smells are the second-largest segment, there are no perfumes we know of based on freshly baked bread or bacon.

We conducted our own survey on Instagram comparing smells that did well in the studies mentioned.[12] We asked our followers about their favorite smells among citrus, just-baked bread, floral, peppermint, bergamot, and freshly cut grass. Just-baked bread came in on top with 36 percent, followed by freshly cut grass at 24 percent, and citrus with 15 percent. Floral, the number one selling segment of the perfume industry, came in second to last.

Just as in the visual world, context matters. What we love in one situation can change in another.

It Tastes and Feels Beautiful

When it comes to describing food, the terms *beautiful* and *gorgeous* are more likely to be used in reference to the visual appearance of a dish—a gorgeous way of plating, a beautiful cut of meat—than to the taste of the dish itself, where descriptors such as *delicious*, *yummy*, and *juicy* are more prevalent.

Similarly, when it comes to touch, popular adjectives might be *soft* or *smooth*, although *your skin feels beautiful* is not an uncommon phrase. The beauty of the popular iPhone Soft Touch cases is also connected to how they feel rather than how they look.

We'd like to create a sensory room that combines experiences for the senses in one single space. We would take into account various research results of people's favorite color, sound, smell, etc. and place the winners of each category into this room. The color of the space would oscillate between yellow and orange (like a sunset), the smell would be citrus-based, and the sound would be generated by Malaysian tree frogs.

Would such a sensual onslaught create a beautiful experience? Would people feel comfortable in such a room? Would it be joyous?

distributor, and retailer. Many high-end designers finance their more experimental haute couture ideas through sales of their perfumes.

and on-the-counter material) at $4, and marketing costs at $8; the remaining $80 pays for overhead and profits for the designer, manufacturer,

* If you take a $100 bottle, the oil responsible for the scent itself is valued at $2, the bottle at $6, the packaging (including fragrance strips

WHICH OF THESE COCA-COLA CANS DO YOU THINK IS THE MOST BEAUTIFUL?

(A)

(B)

(C)

(D)

(E)

(F)

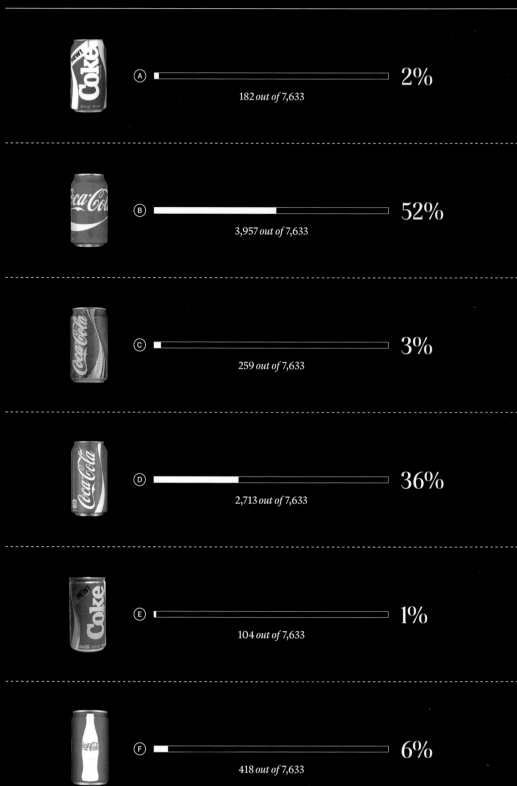

(A) 2%
182 out of 7,633

(B) 52%
3,957 out of 7,633

(C) 3%
259 out of 7,633

(D) 36%
2,713 out of 7,633

(E) 1%
104 out of 7,633

(F) 6%
418 out of 7,633

WHICH OF THESE LOGOS DO YOU THINK IS THE MOST BEAUTIFUL?

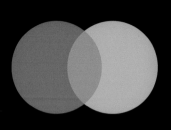

(A)

(B)

(C)

(D)

(E)

(F)

(A) 45%

3,665 *out of* 8,105

(B) 15%

1,173 *out of* 8,105

(C) 2%

164 *out of* 8,105

(D) 17%

1,413 *out of* 8,105

FedEx (E) 10%

792 *out of* 8,105

THE MET (F) 11%

898 *out of* 8,105

1. Wil S. Hylton, "The Mysterious Metamorphosis of Chuck Close," New York Times Magazine, July 13, 2016.

2. Jonathan Glancey, "I Pick up My Pen, a Building Appears," The Guardian, August 1, 2007, https://www.theguardian.com/artanddesign/2007/aug/01/architecture. "Walter Gropius came to see me at my house at Canoas, above Rio. I designed it in a sequence of natural curves to flow in and out of the existing landscape. He said, 'It's beautiful, but it can't be mass-produced.' As if I had intended such a thing! What an idiot."

3. Pascal-Emmanuel Gobry, "Steve Jobs, and the Modern Hunger for Beauty," The Week, October 9, 2015.

4. "A Conversation That Might Have Taken Place," with Louise Schouwenberg, 2003, http://www.jongeriuslab.com.

5. We got the coins back, poured them into little bags, and left them at the site next to a large sign explaining that they were free for anybody to take.

6. Survey was posted on Instagram July 15, 2017.

7. Survey was posted on Instagram July 31, 2017.

8. Survey was posted on Instagram July 4, 2017.

9. Here is a long diary account of Stefan's first meeting with Mick Jagger: On Wednesday, a brand-new and extra-clean stretch limo picks me up at the studio, we are going to Newark airport, the driver hands over business-class tickets for LA, and I have a stupid grin on my face all the way to the airport, looking out over the New Jersey industrial landscape with the Statue of Liberty in my back, contemplating if this is one of those "happy" moments that I have about once a year. Next morning Jagger's assistant Lucy meets me in the bar, gives me a quick rundown on Mick, and we go to the suite. In the elevator, I'm nervous. Mick opens the door, turns around immediately without saying hello, and I feel awkward. Lucy introduces us, he's friendly but busy going through a Sotheby's catalogue with Charlie Watts. "At nine million that's a real bargain," he says in heavy British accent looking at a Monet painting. "Pity I have no walls left to hang it." I help Lucy opening the water bottles, Mick grabs my portfolio and says, "So, you're the floaty one." "The floaty one?" "Yeah, all your covers seem to float in the plastic box." He likes the Lou Reed package, likes the attention to detail in some of the others, and I can stop being nervous. I ask him about his favorite Stones covers, and he mentions without hesitation: Exile on Main Street, Sticky Fingers, and Some Girls. These are my favorites, as well: "We should have an easy time working together since I would have told you exactly the same covers, only in a different order: Sticky Fingers, Some Girls, and Exile on Main Street." Charlie Watts (in lowered voice) asks Jagger: "What's on the Sticky Fingers?" to which Mick replies, "Oh, you know, Charlie, the one with the zipper, the one that Andy did." The stupid happy grin is back on my face.

10. Rafi Haddad, Abebe Medhanie, Yehudah Roth, David Harel, and Noam Sobel, "Predicting Odor Pleasantness with an Electronic Nose," PLoS Computational Biology 6, no. 4 (2010), doi: 10.1371/journal.pcbi.1000740.

11. "Freshly Baked Bread, Bacon, and Freshly Cut Grass: Our Top 50 Favourite Smells Revealed (and the 20 Worst)," Daily Mail, May 25, 2015, http://www.dailymail.co.uk/news/article-3096334/Our-50-favourite-smells-revealed-20-worst.html.

12. Survey was posted on Instagram February 8, 2018.

Pt. —

The Eye of

IV

Beholder

T he most damning argument against beauty as a goal is the notion that it lies in the eye of the beholder. If everyone uses different criteria and subjective experiences to define and identify beauty, setting it as a goal for design, architecture, and the arts is a fruitless endeavor. Any discussion on the subject comes to a halt.

The expression *beauty is in the eye of the beholder* was not minted by an ancient philosopher. It did not result from a wide-ranging survey on aesthetics. It came into our world through a romantic comedy. It was uttered by one of Margaret Wolfe Hungerford's characters in her nineteenth-century novel *Molly Bawn*. But let's not forget that novels are fiction, and this statement isn't true, regardless of how often it is quoted, or where.

In an effort to combat fiction with fact, we have read and conducted surveys, and explored a variety of research, all of which repeatedly proves that all eyes see beauty when it is truly there.

Can Someone Explain Why They Still Sell Brown Suits?

We presented a color survey to our Instagram followers and received more than 6,500 responses![1] (It's rare to receive such a high rate of response to any kind of survey.) Our followers are 50 percent female and 50 percent male.[2]

The results (see p. 120) correlate with a survey conducted by University of Maryland sociologist Dr. Philip Cohen, who asked two thousand of his students the same question. Blue came in first, "followed by green for men and purple for women." His survey results include data sorted by gender, and while males prefer blue by a wider margin, women selected it for their first choice, as well.[3] A worldwide survey by YouGov also came up with blue in first place and brown last.[4]

We asked our Instagram group another question: Which shade of blue (Egyptian blue, light blue, electric blue, baby blue, midnight blue, or periwinkle) do you think is the most beautiful (see p. 122)?[5] Light blue came in first place. Can we deduce from this that light blue is the world's favorite, and therefore most beautiful, color?*

Brown, on the other hand, is the least favorite color. But can we identify the shade of brown that is the world's least favorite (and ugliest)?† We asked followers to rank six frequently used browns by preference (see p. 125).[6] This survey on Instagram received 2,120 likes (as opposed to the 3,650 likes received for our shades-of-blue survey). It also attracted far fewer participants: only 4,746 people responded. Although this number is still statistically significant, it is far fewer people than the 7,624 who voted for their favorite shade of blue.

Our Instagram followers, an admittedly design-conscious crowd, voted for classic brown as their least favorite. From this we can deduce that classic brown is possibly the ugliest color in the world.‡

We also ran a survey on shapes (see pp. 123–24).[7] Almost every other person chose the circle as their favorite, and about a third preferred the round wiggle, while only two in one hundred preferred the rectangle.

We then tested these same shapes as three-dimensional forms, and the results were essentially the same, though slightly more pronounced (see pp. 143–44).[8] Half of all participants preferred the sphere, and the rectangular volume came in last.

The least popular shape is the rectangular volume. The least popular color is classic brown. So, is a classic-brown rectangular volume the ugliest thing possible?§

Ironically, the brown box has been the most dominant shape in architecture over the last hundred years. Surely there are practical reasons to design and build using rectangular shapes. But if you look at historic architecture—from almost any culture—the rectangle

† Yes, yes, we know, technically it is the least favorite among the choices we offered up for selection.

* Yes, we know, technically it is the favorite among the choices we offered up for selection.

DO YOU THINK IS THE MOST BEAUTIFUL?

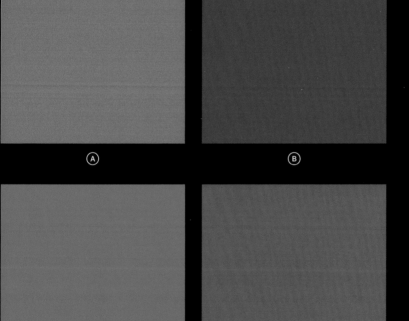

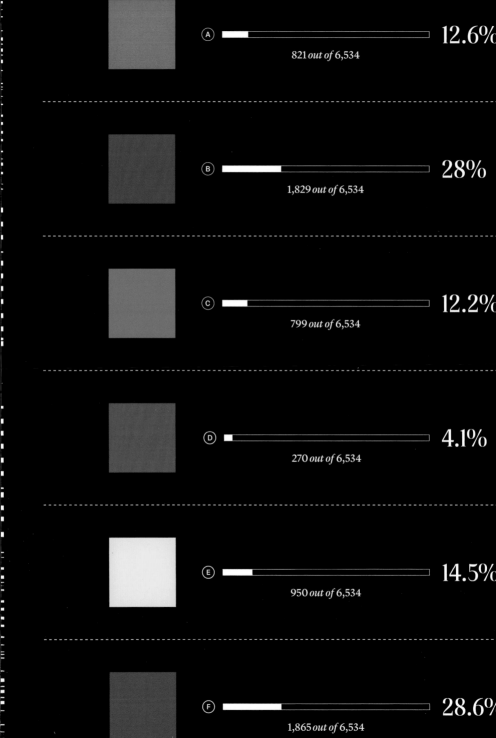

plays a less significant role, while the more popular shapes selected in our own survey are more dominant.

Examples of historic architecture that do not look like boxes

Did Modernism Go Down the Wrong Path?

Dr. Helmut Leder's research confirms that we prefer round objects over sharply angled ones. It would be difficult and impractical to build perfectly spherical structures, but the example of Edwin Lipburger's Kugelmugel house shows that a spherical building can generate widespread admiration.

If the circle is the most beautiful, are other round shapes just as appealing? Of course we asked (see p. 142).[9] Here are the results: the perfect circle rules!

Edwin Lipburger's Kugelmugel house in Austria

My Beautiful Money

Our Instagram followers are equally divided between the United States and Europe. Among the nations represented, a small number of followers live in Switzerland. Familiarity with the currency and, possibly, patriotism would seem to factor into the results when we asked our Instagram community which currency they found the most beautiful.[10]

The euro is the favorite (see pp. 145–46). A scientific survey would adjust for the fact that far fewer Swiss people voted compared to participants from other parts of the eurozone and the United States. Had all three voted in equal number, the Swiss franc would likely have assumed the top position. Beauty seems to have beat out patriotism and familiarity.

Jessica was unsure of her commitment to graphic design after her first year of study at the Rhode Island School of Design. Most of what professors taught stemmed from the International Style; the students spent months perfecting grids and tracing modernist typography, and the examples that the design professors hailed as perfection seemed boring and lacking soul. It was Ootje Oxenaar's class that made her hopeful about design. He would show his beautiful work and explain how he'd interject playfulness and the personal into everything he made. He designed the Dutch banknotes from the 1960s to the '80s, which were kept in circulation until they

WHICH SHADE OF BLUE DO YOU THINK IS THE MOST BEAUTIFUL?

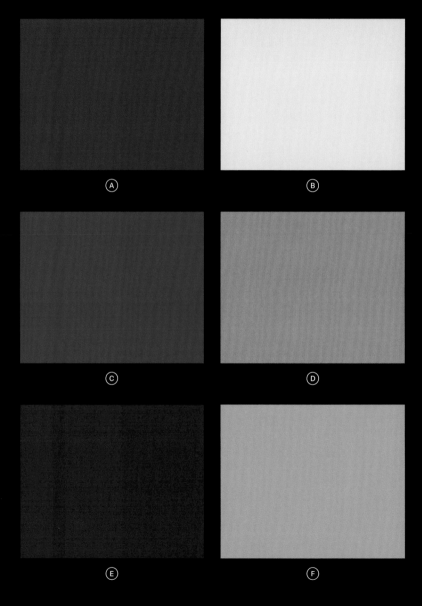

WHICH OF THESE SHAPES DO YOU THINK IS THE MOST BEAUTIFUL?

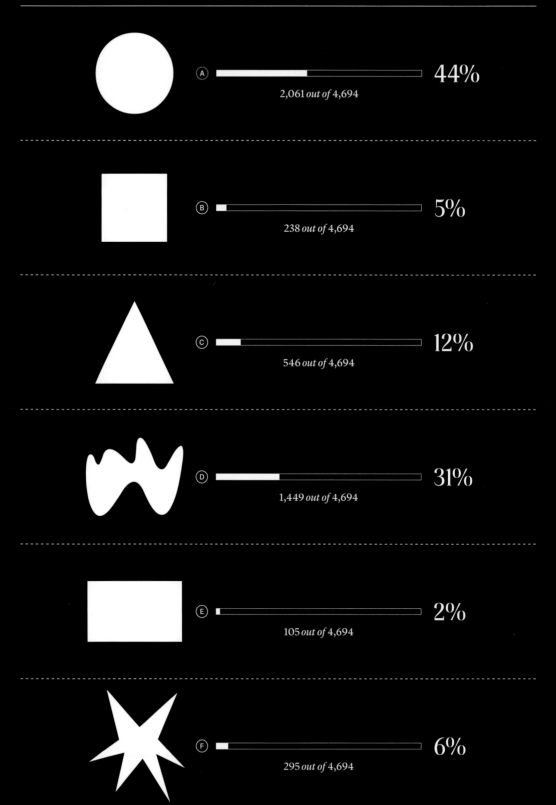

(A) 44%
2,061 out of 4,694

(B) 5%
238 out of 4,694

(C) 12%
546 out of 4,694

(D) 31%
1,449 out of 4,694

(E) 2%
105 out of 4,694

(F) 6%
295 out of 4,694

WHICH SHADE OF BROWN DO YOU THINK IS THE MOST BEAUTIFUL?

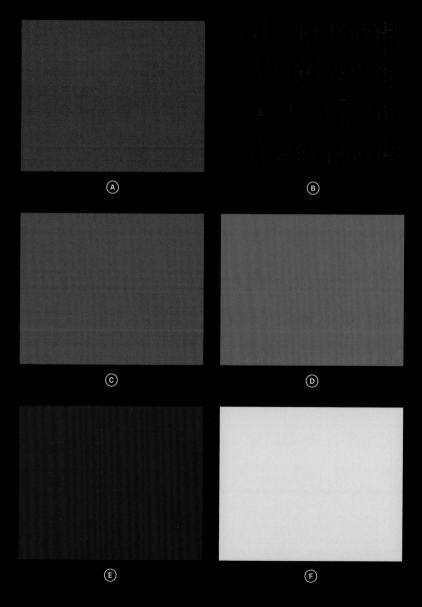

A   B

C   D

E   F

In our survey, 35% found E the most beautiful, 24% D, 16% C, 11% F.
Only 7% found A and 7% found B the most beautiful.

The brown rectangle emerges as the ugliest thing.

*How does the
field of architecture
react to this?*

*If your task is to design a building next to the ugly brown one,
you create a mirrored facade to double the atrocity.*

were replaced by euros. They are beautiful, and when you look closely, each bill contains something personal from Oxenaar's life: the imprint of his middle finger, a drawing of his girlfriend's pet rabbit, or his granddaughter's name. She remembers him giggling with joy at the idea that he was giving his middle finger to everyone in the Netherlands, realizing there was more to design than perfect kerning.

We also thought familiarity and patriotism would factor into voting about the relative beauty of passports, making the final results all the more remarkable (see pp. 147–48).[11]

Even though we know there are few Swiss voters among our Instagram followers, the Swiss passport was considered the most attractive by more than three-quarters of all respondents. When there is international consensus, how can beauty be in the eye of the beholder?

The Ten Most Beautiful Cities in the World

—

When we compared surveys of which cities people consider the world's most beautiful, the same names came up again and again (see p. 135).[12] We have visited all ten of these lovely places and can confirm that the surveys are correct: these are truly beautiful cities. Some stand out for their architecture, some for how they're situated within nature, but all are absolutely stunning. Unfortunately, whenever we visit, it turns out that people from all the ugly places in the world have also been attracted by the beauty, overcrowding these spots and considerably diminishing the enjoyment of said beauty.

"One Entered the City Like a God. One Scuttles in Now Like a Rat."[13]

—

Researchers at the New England Complex Systems Institute (NECSI), a research facility studying complex data, created a mood map of New York City using data from Twitter. They developed a simple algorithm that can detect if a tweeted message is, overall, negative or positive. Using this tool, they're able to determine how people feel anywhere in the city. If an area is shaded green, more positive messages emit from this place; if it is red, more negative messages are sent.

Let's compare two transportation hubs: Grand Central Terminal, a grand, 1913 building by the architecture firms Reed & Stem and Warren & Wetmore, and Penn Station, a dark, underground hub built in the late 1960s.

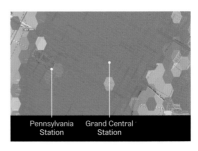

On the mood map, Grand Central is always green, while Penn Station is always red. But you don't need the NECSI to come to this realization. On your next visit to Manhattan, make the brisk, twenty-minute walk from one station to the other and you'll see the difference in the travelers' moods. Those moving through Grand Central are always—at any time, night or day—in noticeably better moods than those in Penn Station.

We took a look at some of the individual tweets coming out of each station. Here are a few from Grand Central:

The messages coming out of Penn Station are rather different:

And people don't just feel different in these stations, they also behave differently.

Small Is Beautiful.
Diversity Is Beautiful.

—

Dr. Colin Ellard, a neuroscientist at the University of Waterloo and director of its Urban Realities Laboratory, asked people walking down Houston Street in New York City to wear electronic bracelets so he could measure their feelings. In front of the giant Whole Foods Market, situated in a humdrum, glass-facade building on the corner of the Bowery, participants wearing the bracelets were physiologically manifesting signs of boredom. Asked to describe their reactions to this particular spot, they used words like *bland*, *monotonous*, and *passionless*.

**The Whole Foods Market on
East Houston Street in New York**

In contrast, one block east of the Whole Foods on East Houston, at the other test site—a "lively sea of restaurants with lots of open doors and windows"—people's bracelets measured high levels of physical excitement, and participants listed words such as *lively*, *busy*, and *socializing* to describe the area.[14]

Ellard's research makes clear that we favor diversity over monotony, that we feel more alive in an environment featuring a mixture of buildings and styles.

**One block farther east, on East Houston
Street, the storefront of Russ & Daughters**

No wonder one of our favorite parts of the city is the West Village. The winding streets have unexpected shops, restaurants, and architecture at every turn. We're not alone in this thinking: its charming appeal makes it one of the most expensive real estate neighborhoods in the city.

Such findings could have far-reaching impacts on the commissioning and planning of architectural projects. For instance, when the campus of the new University of Economics and Business in Vienna was commissioned under the master plan of architect Laura Spindel, the job was not given to a single architectural firm, but instead divided among six firms, each assigned a distinct section. This resulted in a dynamic feeling on campus right from the start. We visited the campus three months after its opening, and it already felt lived-in—the public spaces were teeming with students. It worked. It was alive.

Going Away and
Never Leaving

—

If we fly from Athens to Bangkok, through Sapporo to Sofia, we'd better double-check our boarding passes to see where we are—we would not get a clue from the architecture of

*The Ten Most Beautiful Metropolises
in the World:*

*Rome, Paris,
Prague,
Rio de Janeiro,
Kyoto,
Cape Town,
Saint Petersburg,
Vienna,
San Francisco &
Barcelona*

*Whenever
we visit one
of these
beautiful cities,
all the
people from the
ugly places
around
the world are
also there.*

Athens

Sapporo

Brussels

Sochi

these airports. Considering the significant cultural differences between Greece, Thailand, Japan, and Bulgaria and the vast possibilities these travel hubs offer for creating a sense of place, it's mind-boggling that they're designed within the exact same parameters. These airports make you feel as though you never left in the first place. We might have just traveled more than ten thousand miles, but aesthetically and culturally, we're still in the same building.

In fact, we often don't realize where we've landed until we try to recharge our phones and notice that the plug won't fit! Apparently, electricians never adopted the International Style.

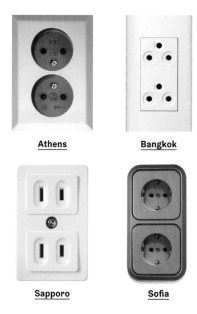

Athens	**Bangkok**
Sapporo	**Sofia**

This problem is exacerbated in American airports, which are often value-engineered into soul-crushing environments that amplify the usual frustrations of air travel. Long lines are ubiquitous, delays the norm.

We spoke with an executive at the excellent Haneda Airport in Tokyo, who stated that if we see a long line of people at an airport today, something is wrong. Crowd prediction software has become so sophisticated that it should be possible for any airport to move people efficiently without increasing the number of staff. It turns out that the people who insist on the supremacy of sameness under the guise of functionalism frequently don't use the software that would actually make things work.

Does Sameness Work Better?
–

Let's look at subway systems. The example we're using here is from Munich, but we could have chosen any subway system built in the mid- to late twentieth century. Many appear to follow the same strategy of color coding within a narrow set of formal parameters. Each line is assigned a particular color for identification and signage, and every station along that route is marked with the assigned color.

When traveling from Hauptbahnhof to Karl-Preis-Platz, Theresienstraße to Messestadt Ost, or Fraunhoferstraße to Giesing, one always remains within the exact same visual system. We assumed that this universal design strategy, this sameness, would get us from A to B in the most efficient manner.

That is, until we visited Moscow. There, every station is unique—different colors, different surfaces in different materials and patterns, different structures and architectural styles. In the Moscow subway system, we can check our phones, read a book, or just daydream and we will know, intuitively, when we arrive at our destination.[15] We don't have to squint to figure out a fragment of Helvetica behind a column to know we've arrived.

The Moscow system *works* better.

We also noticed that at every station in Moscow a large group of people get out of the train, quickly take pictures in the station, and then get back into their compartments. They repeat this ritual at every stop. Moscow's subway system has become a tourist attraction.

In Munich, we were the only ones with our cameras out.

WHICH OF THESE SHAPES DO YOU THINK IS THE MOST BEAUTIFUL?

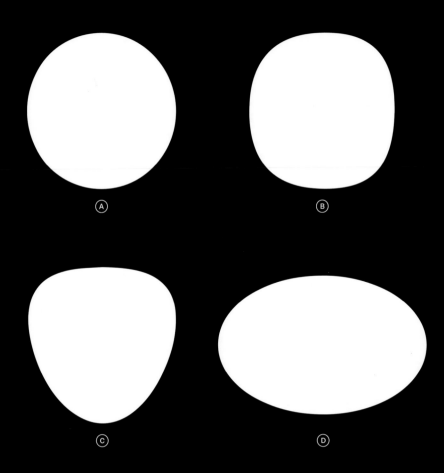

In our survey, 35% found A the most beautiful, 32% C, and 28% B.
Only 5% found D the most beautiful.

WHICH OF THESE FORMS DO YOU THINK IS THE MOST BEAUTIFUL?

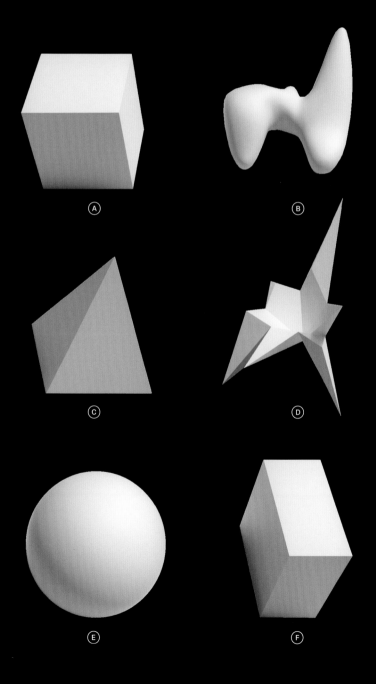

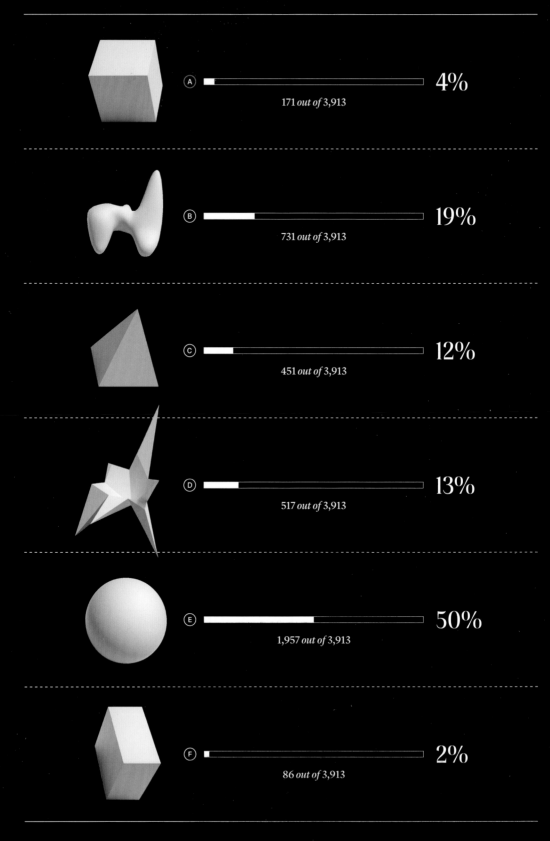

(A) 4%
171 *out of* 3,913

(B) 19%
731 *out of* 3,913

(C) 12%
451 *out of* 3,913

(D) 13%
517 *out of* 3,913

(E) 50%
1,957 *out of* 3,913

(F) 2%
86 *out of* 3,913

(B)

(A) ████████████░░░░░░░░░░░░░░ 43%

2,256 *out of* 5,290

(B) ███░░░░░░░░░░░░░░░░░░░░░░░ 12%

638 *out of* 5,290

(C) ████████████░░░░░░░░░░░░░░ 45%

2,396 *out of* 5,290

Schweizer Pass
Passeport suisse
Passaporto svizzero
Passaport svizzer
Swiss passport

PASSPORT

United States
of America

REISEPASS

PASSPORT

(A)

5,292 *out of* 6,642

(B)

917 *out of* 6,642

(C)

433 *out of* 6,642

1. The exact question posed on Instagram was: "For a project on beauty, we'll be conducting a little research: Which of these colors do you like best? Please respond by commenting with a number."

2. The survey was posted on Instagram March 12, 2017. The 6,534 participants were from around the world—30 percent from the United States, 15 percent from the United Kingdom, 10 percent from Germany, 7 percent from Brazil, 7 percent from Mexico, and 31 percent from other countries—and were almost evenly split among males (51 percent) and females (49 percent).

3. Natalie Wolchover, "Pie Chart: Humanity's Favorite Colors," LiveScience.com, July 31, 2012, https://www.livescience.com/34105-favorite-colors.html.

4. William Jordan, "Why Is Blue the World's Favorite Color?" YouGov, May 12, 2015, https://today.yougov.com/news/2015/05/12/why-blue-worlds-favorite-color/.

5. Survey was posted on Instagram March 31, 2017. Light blue is RGB 173/216/230 and CMYK 30/3/4/0.

6. Survey was posted on Instagram May 1, 2017.

7. Survey was posted on Instagram March 23, 2017.

8. Survey was posted on Instagram April 14, 2017.

9. Survey was posted on Instagram May 11, 2017.

10. Survey was posted on Instagram April 5, 2017. The only countries that preferred the US bill were Malaysia and Greece. Most of Europe preferred the Swiss franc. Most of the Americas preferred the euro (including the US). Switzerland notoriously preferred their franc, but so did most of Europe. Only 7 percent of US followers liked their own money—that's one of the lowest percentages among all countries.

11. Survey was posted on Instagram June 1, 2017.

12. See Kerstin Schmidt, "The World's Most Beautiful Cities," Conde Nast Traveler, October 23, 2015; Mark Kahler, "Top 10 Most Beautiful Cities in the World," in Let's Roll, a blog by FlightNetwork, April 13, 2016; and Tim Kiladze, "World's Most Beautiful Cities," Forbes, January 22, 2010.

13. Vincent Scully quoted in Herbert Muschamp, "Architecture View: In This Dream Station, Future and Past Collide," New York Times, June 20, 1993.

14. Colin Ellard, Places of the Heart: The Psychogeography of Everyday Life (New York: Bellevue Literary Press, 2015), 108–9.

15. A decade after the October Revolution, the government wanted to build subway stations as "palaces for the people"; the very best architects were recruited, each to design an individual station.

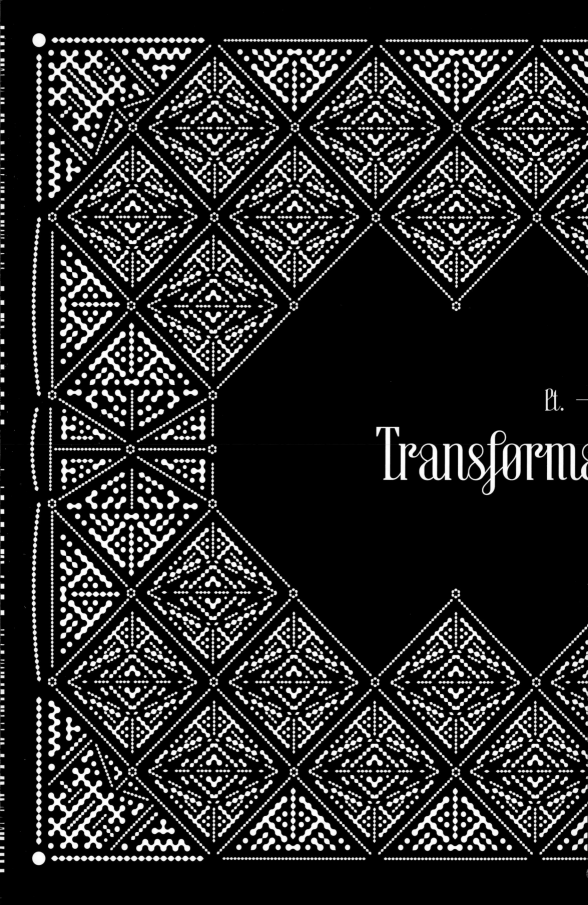

Pt. —

Transforma

— V

onal Beauty

B eauty can transform us. It can change how we feel, and it can change how we behave. It can influence our decisions on where to spend our holidays and where we invest our money, and it can impact our willingness to pay taxes. When a public place becomes noticeably neglected, littering and vandalism rise exponentially.

A neglected underpass located below the Brooklyn-Queens Expressway was regularly used as a late-night toilet by guys coming out of the neighborhood bars. It smelled bad.

A neglected underpass below
the BQE in Brooklyn

One of our clients wanted to do something about it and had a modest budget of $5,000 to spend on a solution. We had no intention of posting a large sign saying, "Dear guys, do not pee here," but weren't able to create something much more ambitious than painting the walls. Since the underpass is shared by cars, bikes, and pedestrians—all traveling through at different speeds—we needed to design something that could be read quickly by people passing by fast and slow.

An elaborate *yes* on one wall
of the underpass

So we painted a rather elaborate *yes* on one wall of the underpass, providing pedestrians with something to look at, and a simple graphic *yes* on the other, which would also be legible to passengers riding in cars.

Because of the large *yes*, newlyweds began using the underpass as a backdrop for wedding photos. With $5,000, we transformed a toilet into a wedding chapel.

Nature Turns into a Landscape
-

Human beings have always strived to transform their surroundings into more enjoyable, livable, and beautiful spaces. While we often get caught up in considering the damage we've inflicted on nature, there are plenty of examples where human presence has increased the existing beauty. If we consider three of the places Stefan has lived—Bali, the Bregenzer Wald in Austria, and Hong Kong—all have been aesthetically improved by agricultural or urban development.

The transformation of nature into
landscape: Indonesia

How We Feel
-

For centuries, people have visited Cimitero Monumentale del Verano in the center of

Because of the large yes, newlyweds started to use the underpass as a backdrop for wedding photos.

TRANSFORMATIONAL BEAUTY

TRANSFORMATIONAL BEAUTY

Rome and placed flowers onto its beautifully carved headstones. There, beauty supports the expression of emotion and provides a consoling space for grief.

American art critic Arthur Danto writes that beauty can help "the tears to flow...putting the loss into a certain philosophical perspective."[1]

Although the Roman cemetery is sometimes devoid of visitors, the effort to ease pain through beauty exists in spontaneous memorials, small and large, created in the wake of traumatic events, including terrorist attacks. These memorials appeared in large numbers after 9/11 in New York, and after the 2015 and 2017 attacks in Paris and London, respectively. They have similarly sprung up in the wake of the deaths of beloved public figures, such as Princess Diana and David Bowie.

Small ad-hoc memorials: easing pain through beauty

A memorial should be a space that keeps us from suffering alone. It should enable people to share their grief and acknowledge loss as a community of mourners. Michael Arad's 9/11 memorial in New York City facilitates the formation of such a community.

The enormous waterfalls that stand in the footprints of the fallen towers of the World Trade Center create such a thundering roar that the sirens and traffic noise of downtown

Michael Arad's 9/11 memorial in New York

Manhattan fall away, making contemplation possible. The memorial conveys a solemn message: something important used to be here and now is gone. But things are flowing, time moves on, life continues.

The National September 11 Memorial is a beautiful space where silence roars. It is smack in the center of one of the most expensive real estate parcels in the world, an idyll that lacks functionality, an area that will never sell condos or office space. It just *is*. And that is especially beautiful.

Transforming Spaces and Buildings
–

Manchester Bidwell Corporation, founded by Bill Strickland, is a training institution in fields as diverse as horticulture, the culinary arts, and medicine. Strickland was convinced that beauty would have an influence on the people he trained—regardless of socioeconomic standing—and he filled his centers with fresh flowers, art objects, and well-designed furniture.

He also placed a fountain in the lobby of his first building. "At a reception in [a prominent museum's] courtyard, I noticed that they had a fountain because they think that the people who go to the museum deserve a fountain. Well, I think that welfare mothers and at-risk kids and ex-steel workers deserve a fountain in their life."[2] Strickland has since established centers in Cleveland; Buffalo; New

TRANSFORMATIONAL BEAUTY

Haven, Connecticut; Cincinnati; Grand Rapids, Michigan; Brockway, Pennsylvania; and San Francisco, teaching skills in the culinary and visual arts to thousands of students.

The High Line

—

Originally built as an elevated track in the 1930s to carry cargo trains to Manhattan factories, the High Line was all function and little beauty.

The High Line in 1930

The High Line's tracks served their purpose for almost fifty years, until they were abandoned in the 1980s as industry left the city. When the line fell into disrepair, the small downtown population who'd settled among the body shops and parking garages on Manhattan's West Side saw it as a hulking blight, blocking out much of the light on Tenth Avenue.

The High Line in 1990

The site was destined for demolition until community organizers Robert Hammond and Joshua David came along and saw potential in the elevated train track to create a

new kind of public outdoor space in the city. Together they put lots of love and care into its resurrection. Hammond and David organized an architectural competition, won by Diller Scofidio + Renfro, who transformed the steel construction into the now almost universally loved elevated park. It invigorated the neighborhood of West Chelsea, triggering billions of dollars in new construction from Twelfth Street all the way to Thirty-Fourth Street, and will likely emerge as one of the most influential architectural transformations in Manhattan in a generation. As this book goes to press, there are more than sixty projects around the world already built or in the planning stages that take their design cues directly from the High Line.[3] Interesting, too, is the fact that the excellent design and renovation of the High Line seems to have set the bar for many of the buildings that have gone up alongside it; these new constructions seem more carefully considered than elsewhere in New York City.*

Buildings adjoining the High Line seem more carefully considered than elsewhere in New York City.

The power of great design shows up in ways that may not have been intended. In the case of the High Line, we see the effects of this beautiful structure on the behavior of its users. Every morning at seven o'clock, Stefan runs its length and is surprised by the complete lack of litter. Not once on his runs has there ever been a piece of paper or an empty can on the ground. Only several feet away, in the Meatpacking District, however, garbage

* The majority of the new buildings constructed next to the High Line are luxury condominiums.

abounds. Even more impressive is an article by the *New York Times* that two years after its opening, no major crime on the High Line had been reported.[4]

The High Line in 2017

In another instance of an imaginative strategy, our friend Bjarke Ingels of the architectural firm BIG is in the process of designing a large-scale project in Vancouver with great potential to transform its current site. Ingels was asked to design a tower on a challenging site abutting a heavily trafficked highway. He decided to transform the neglected space underneath the highway into a covered outdoor market. His strategy will provide shelter to pedestrians while they shop, hang out, and

BIG's planned transformation of a neglected space into a covered outdoor market in Vancouver

enjoy cultural activities. This shelter will likely prove to be a wonderful resource in a city where it rains more than 160 days each year. The plan includes covering the underside of the highway with photography by local artists, creating what Ingels calls the "Sistine Chapel of street art."

Nonspaces and Junk Spaces
-

Even universally acknowledged beautiful cities such as Rome and Prague feature a plethora of highway off-ramps, sound-protection walls, strip malls, and industrial zones that are, essentially, aesthetic blights governed by functionalism. The world is filled with these nonspaces, which seem to grow as if by themselves, multiplying in and around towns, often initiated by planners and builders without the involvement of architects. So why not fill these spaces with beauty? Imaginative design might transform a neglected parking lot into a joyous location. Surely these unsightly spaces can be reworked so that people actually want to spend time in them, or at the very least won't mind having to pass through them.

The Curious Case of Friedensreich Hundertwasser
-

In the 1980s, the Austrian artist Friedensreich Hundertwasser turned his attention to architecture, specifically public housing projects and churches, with an eye to transforming industrial structures. Hundertwasser took a waste incineration plant and decorated its chimney with golden balls, added colorful columns, and covered it with his signature ornamental elements. Architects denounced the results, and he became the laughingstock of the intelligentsia. Stefan was an art student at the University of Applied Arts in Vienna at the time and remembers everyone hating Hundertwasser's work. It was quintessentially *uncool*.

TRANSFORMATIONAL BEAUTY

This spread and following:
imaginative design can transform junk spaces.

Roughly thirty years later, we see the situation differently. A standard waste-incineration plant from the '80s looks very grim compared to Hundertwasser's creation. Outside academic, architecture, and art circles, people have grown to appreciate his work—his industrial plant has become a fixture on many city tours.

Compared to Hundertwasser's concoction, a standard waste-incineration plant from the '80s looks grim.

A City as a Coloring Book

—

During the second half of the twentieth century, Albanians lived under a formidably restrictive communist regime. When the Eastern bloc collapsed, Albania became one of the poorest, most corrupt, and most dysfunctional countries in the former Soviet Union.

Edi Rama was the son of a highly respected artist who worked during the communist era. He showed early talent and moved to Paris to start his own successful career. When Rama returned to his hometown of Tirana, Albania's capital, for his father's funeral, the city was in terrible shape, while cities in neighboring countries had vastly improved. He stayed to help, and became involved in politics. Ultimately, Rama accepted an offer to become minister of culture, and in 2000, he ran successfully for mayor of Tirana.

The city was still in appalling shape, with block after block of crumbling, gray, Soviet-style buildings. There was no money in the municipal coffers to repair or rebuild, but Rama managed to secure funding from Germany and used it to paint Tirana in color. Some inhabitants loved their newly colorful city, while others hated it, prompting him to hold a referendum. Sixty percent, it turns out, were in favor of the change. He also demolished

The mayor of the capital of Albania had the city painted in colors.

hundreds of illegal constructions and planted thousands of trees. The changes resulted in a reduction in crime and an uptick in tax revenue as the population felt that the government was finally doing *something*. Tirana also managed to become something of a tourist attraction, unimaginable only a few years earlier.

Rama was reelected twice as Tirana's mayor and received the World Mayor award in 2004. He is now the prime minister of Albania.

A BBQ in Rio
-

Around the time Edi Rama was being celebrated as an innovator of urban renewal, the Dutch designer Jeroen Koolhaas and the artist Dre Urhahn created the Favela Painting project in Rio de Janeiro. They started with a barbecue, inviting the community to share a meal and discuss their project, its goals, and the form it might take. Together with the community, they created paintings integrating buildings, plazas, and streets. The project was met with international praise and became the inspiration for similar projects elsewhere in South America.

A favela in Rio de Janeiro before
the Favela Painting project

Philadelphia Is Full
of Murals
-

The most sophisticated and far-reaching mural project in the United States grew, ironically, out of an anti-graffiti initiative. The Mural Arts was founded in 1984 as an effective and creative way to channel the energy of graffiti artists in a more community-oriented direction. In the last thirty-five years, thousands of murals have been painted in Philadelphia, creating a noticeable impact

The Mural Arts program in Philadelphia:
the most sophisticated and far-reaching
mural project in the United States

on the city and becoming instrumental in transforming many blighted neighborhoods. Under the leadership of artist and community organizer Jane Golden, the program offers tours, community painting projects, tutorials for aspiring painters, and a conference where questions of effectiveness are discussed. The Mural Arts program is one of the largest employers of artists in Philadelphia.

In 2011, Koolhaas and Urhahn, the designer/artist duo who created the Favela Painting project in Rio, moved to Philadelphia to participate in its Mural Arts program.

The Beautiful
Blue City in India
-

Historically, Rajasthan's Brahmins, the highest caste in India, painted their houses blue as a reference to Lord Shiva. This was also a visual way to communicate their social status. Over the years, people of the lower castes copied them, rationalizing that the blue color would keep mosquitoes away or create a cooler shelter from the hot summer sun. While the effect on mosquitoes is questionable, the visual results are

TRANSFORMATIONAL BEAUTY

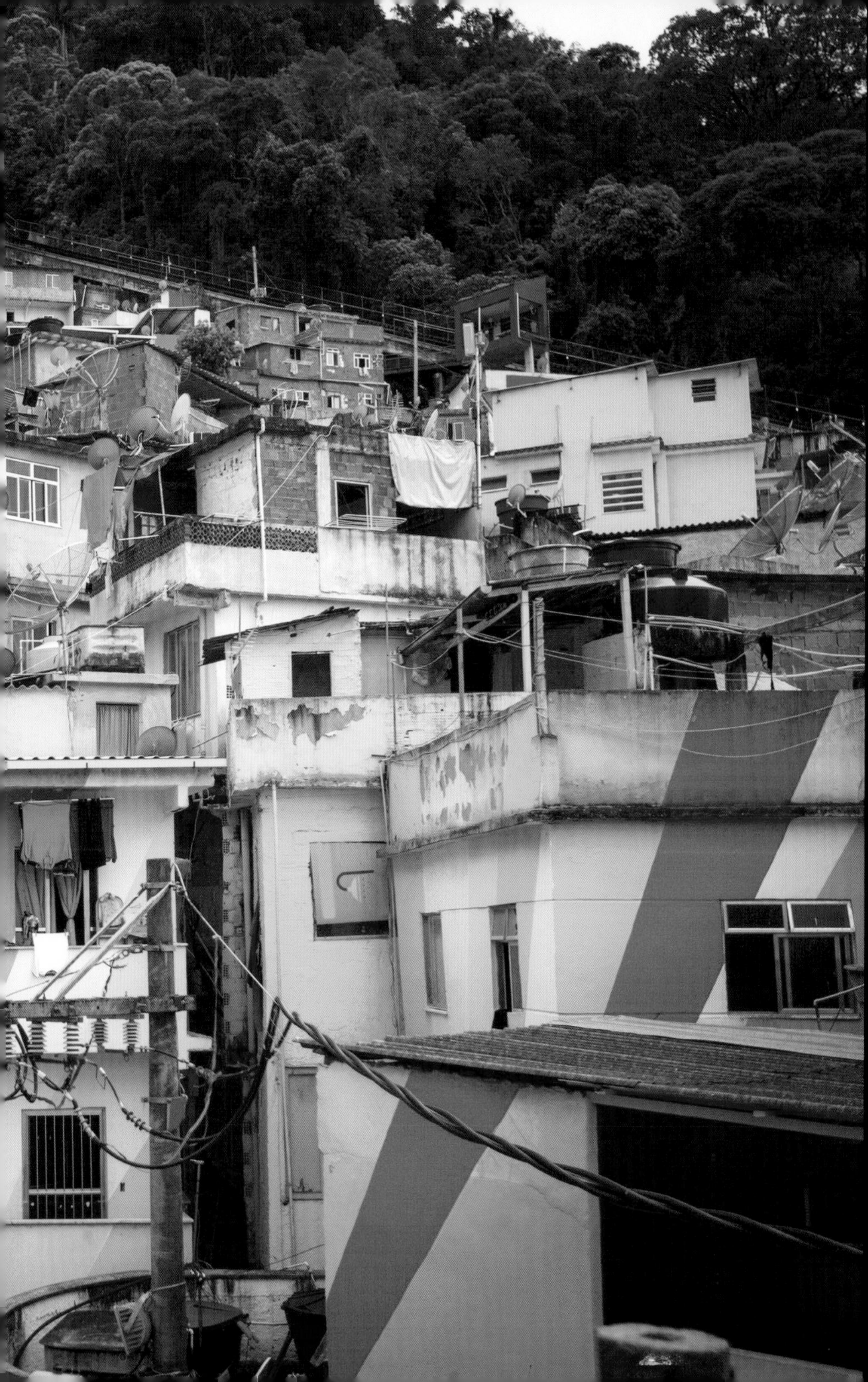

The Favela Painting project in Rio de Janeiro

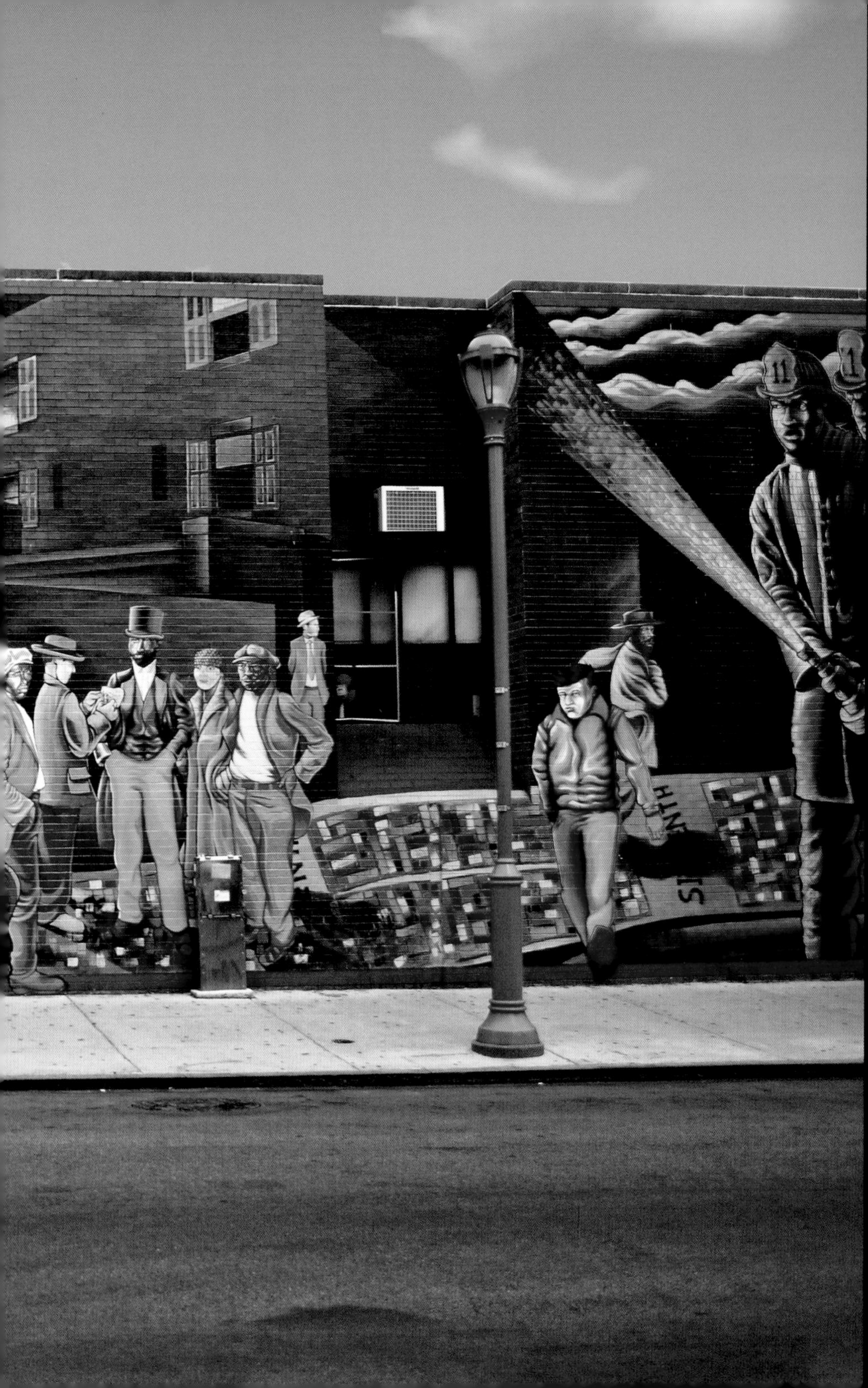

Work created for the Mural Arts program.

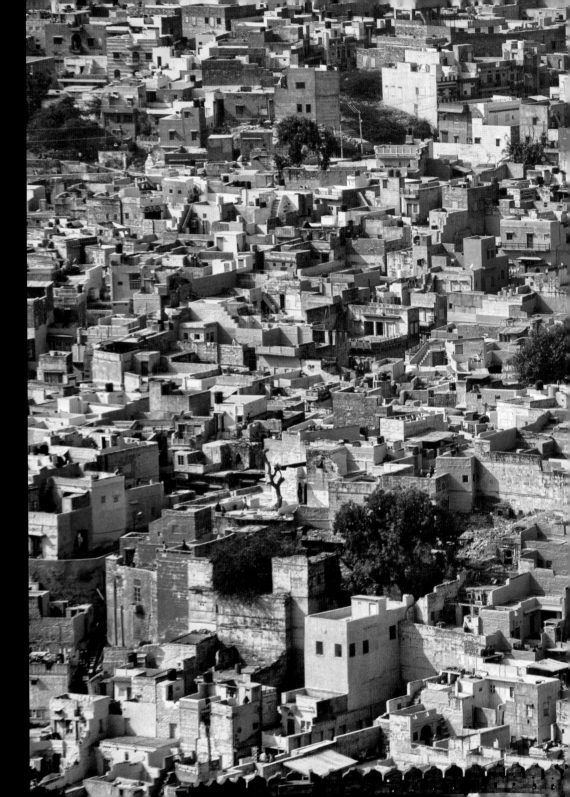

The Blue City of Jodhpur has become one of the main tourist attractions of Rajasthan.

striking, and the city of Jodhpur has become one of the main tourist attractions of Rajasthan. Although the structures themselves are often as simple and unassuming as elsewhere in India, the prevalence and density of color transforms the cityscape into a stunning vista.

Fashion as Landscape Architecture
-

Another element that adds to the visual wonder of Rajasthan requires no expensive updating of infrastructure or costly architectural improvements. It's simply generated by the extremely colorful clothing choices of the population. The red, pink, saffron-yellow, and turquoise fabrics worn by both men and women brighten up life everywhere—from the tiniest villages to the largest cities. The only drably dressed people are tourists in khaki shorts and trekking sandals.

Clothing choices add to the visual wonder of Rajasthan.

No More Billboards in São Paulo
-

Gilberto Kassab, the conservative mayor of São Paulo, instituted a near-total ban on outdoor advertising in 2007, getting rid of thousands of billboards. He also forced companies and institutions to radically reduce the size of their building signs, the scale of the new size determined by a computer formula based on the size of the building's facade. He banned all advertising on buses and taxis in the epicenter of Brazilian commerce and

The mayor of São Paulo instituted a ban on outdoor advertising.

2013. _0
서정민
김세나
엄채송

The Bolivian architect Freddy Mamani transformed El Alto—one of the world's highest cities—with a whole new combination of the indigenous Aymaran style, Art Deco, and Las Vegas–inspired glitz.

made the distribution of flyers illegal. The result was a city largely freed of visual pollution. While the Brazilian advertising industry initially opposed the measures, they changed their minds when agencies realized they could organize painted murals for their clients. These murals, designed and executed by local artists, could focus on a subject close to the advertisers' area of commercial interest as long as they did not feature brand names, logos, slogans, or depictions of products. Today, more than 70 percent of the population approves of the ban and is committed to keeping their city ad-free.

And No Jarring Signage in Quito
—

The example of São Paulo had widespread impact throughout Latin America. The old town of Quito, in Ecuador, pushed it further by insisting that only a certain type of metal sign be used. While this initially met with opposition, once the law went into effect, positive results multiplied. The competition between businesses to create larger and larger signs stopped. Store owners no longer felt the need to waste money on new signs. Since every store displayed the same size sign communicating the kind of offerings that could be found inside, shopping seemed more orderly and efficient to consumers. And of course, the beauty of the historic architecture could be seen and enjoyed.

All signs in the old town of Quito are made out of a specific type of metal.

Quito was declared a UNESCO world heritage site in 1978, but it wasn't until Mayor Paco Moncayo started an extensive restoration program that the historic center was transformed from a largely abandoned and crime-ridden ghetto into a center filled with activities, bustling restaurants, and nightclubs. Quito's residential downtown is dotted with magnificent churches and wonderful hotels.* The city now rivals the Galapagos Islands as a major travel destination in Ecuador.

Soul for Seoul
—

Within Seoul's city limits is Ihwa Mural Village, where more than sixty students and artists revived a decaying hillside suburb using art. What was once a depressed neighborhood with no way to generate income quickly transformed into a popular destination that now attracts international visitors. This increased tourism supported the growth of artisanal businesses, coffee shops, galleries, and tiny bars throughout the village. The paint worked almost too well: locals began to complain about the noise from all the visitors, to the point where they even painted over a few of the murals in the hope that the village's popularity would die down!

The practical efforts of both designers and local residents to enhance the appeal of their cities exemplify our views. The simple act of painting—often using colors that would never receive approval from orthodox Modernists—has triggered significant improvements in the quality of life in a number of emerging cities. The power of beauty to transform life is clear. Our beliefs are not theoretical—they have been proven from Philadelphia to Rio, from Tirana to Seoul.

* The interior of one church is covered in gold leaf.

1. Arthur Danto, <u>The Abuse of Beauty: Aesthetics
    and the Concept of Art</u> (Chicago: Open Court,
    2003), 106.

2. Bill Strickland, "Rebuilding a Neighborhood
    with Beauty, Dignity, Hope," TED2002, February
    2002.

3. "Diller Scofidio + Renfro's Liz Diller in con-
    versation with Stefan Sagmeister," <u>Wallpaper</u>,
    September 30, 2015.

4. Michael Wilson, "The Park Is Elevated. Its
    Crime Rate Is Anything But," <u>New York Times</u>,
    June 10, 2011.

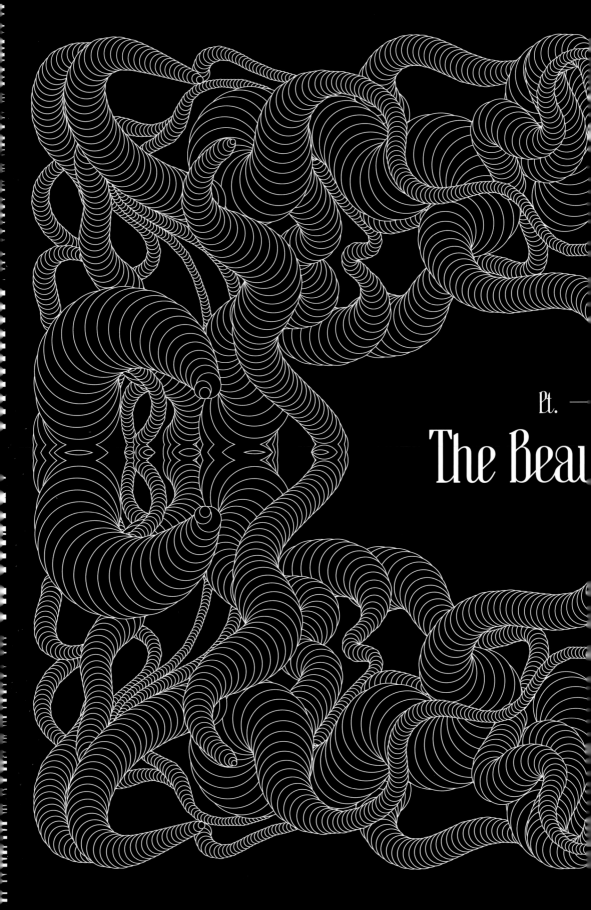

Pt. —

The Beau

VI

Archive

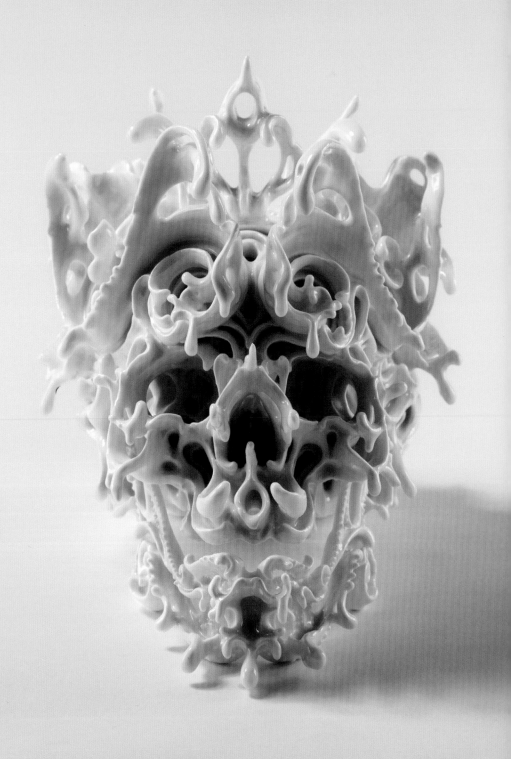

***Predictive Dream XV* (2010) by Katsuyo Aoki**
Aoki is known for her delicate ceramic sculptures, which often depict dark subject matter,
creating an enticing contrast between the grotesque and the beautiful.

T his is an archive we've created of beautiful things. When selecting these pieces, we focused only on their formal qualities. We did not try out a chair to see if it was comfortable, we did not ask an advertiser if a campaign worked, we did not check if a lamp gave off enough light. For a designer, getting things to work is the easy part. It's not hard to design a chair someone can sit on; it doesn't take genius to combine a seat with a backrest and four legs. It does, however, take real talent to produce a chair that's comfortable, attractive, and relevant to its time.

Although we used "beautiful" as the single criterion when choosing the pieces, when we reviewed the objects we'd selected, it turned out that every single one functions perfectly well. The dragon robe increased the status of the Chinese emperor. The Villiger Cigars packaging has successfully protected and sold Swiss *stumpen* (square-cut cigars) for eighty years. Oswald Haerdtl's glasses have been in continuous production for almost a century.

Beauty = Function. It works.

Cabinet (1913) by Dagobert Peche

Peche's cabinet reminds us of how conservatively we furnish our apartments today. This craziness from a hundred years ago features gold patterns on impeccably executed wooden panels, all supported by eight legs.

Milan Cathedral (1386–1965)

We vividly remember attending an Easter mass in this extraordinary Italian cathedral. The entire space was filled with incense smoke. The cone-hatted archbishop was followed by hundreds of bishops, priests, and altar boys, while the light of God streamed through giant windows. The spectacle felt like the start of an epic rock concert. The minds of peasants who made the journey to Milan six hundred years ago must have been blown to smithereens.

Advertisement (1999) by Jason Holley

An illustrator who isn't an expert typographer but incorporates vernacular street typography and tries to get it right: this combination of bee, ice cream, and animal skeleton gets something very right.

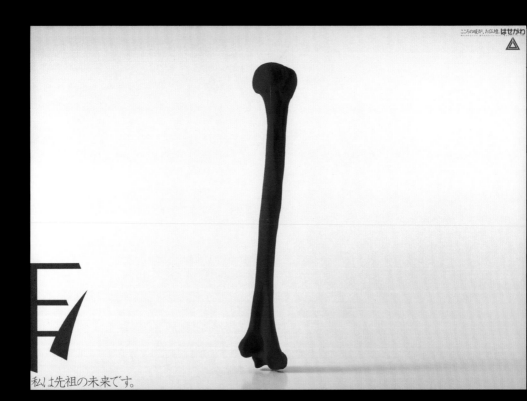

こころの渡橋が、お仏壇 はせがわ

私は先祖の未来です。

Hasegawa Co. Poster (1985) by Makoto Saito
This masterpiece was created by the Japanese star designer Saito for a company selling
Buddhist house altars. With its unusual composition and color, it serves as an early example of how newness
presented in the right context can immediately be seen as beautiful.

Untitled (1989) by Donald Judd
Judd once said that design has to work, art does not. His gorgeous lacquered-aluminum sculpture just _is_.

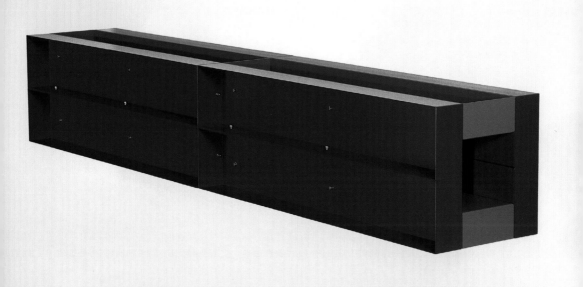

Imperial Dragon Robe (1900–10)

Oh, to be the emperor of China! He employed five hundred artisans to sew and another forty artisans to stitch the gold embroidery.
Then as now, clothing created status; the reign of the emperor was said to have officially begun only after he started wearing this new robe.

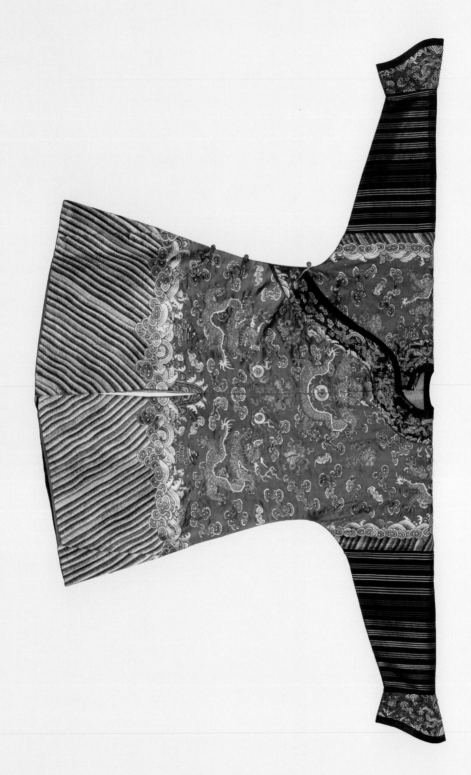

Chauffeuse basse dite Kangourou (c. 1955) by Pierre Jeanneret

The architect Pierre Jeanneret, a cousin of Le Corbusier and also an accomplished furniture designer,
was one of the chief architects of the planned city of Chandigarh in India. He designed a large range of furniture,

San Marco Basilica (828–1094)
The floor of Venice's famed basilica is covered with the rarest marbles from the Eastern world. It is almost one thousand years old, and we think a more beautiful floor has not been made since.

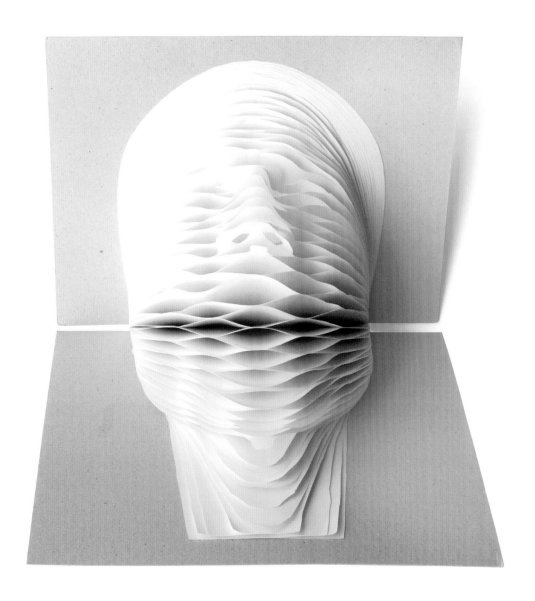

<u>Card (2006) by Simon Oosterdijk</u>

Adapting a technique popularized by birthday celebrations, this festive version of the human form
unfolds from a simple card.

Etui for Meissen Cup and Saucer (1801–33)

Here's an example of when the packaging itself is as beautiful as the object it contains: a small leather and wood case for a nineteenth-century porcelain cup and saucer.

City Palace, Jaipur, India (1729–32)

During her honeymoon, Jessica traveled through Rajasthan. One of her favorite stops was City Palace in Jaipur, a palace complex built by Sawai Jai Singh II. The building is exquisitely decorated with mirror work, mosaics, intricate ornamentation, and paintings.

Metamorphosis Insectorum Surinamensium (1705) by Maria Sibylla Merian

Merian began collecting insects as a young girl, which was a controversial hobby in the seventeenth century, considering that insects were seen as disgusting at best, and at worst, related to witchcraft. Rather than ending up burned to a crisp, she went to Suriname on a research trip to collect the creatures in order to study and draw them.

Meissen Porcelain Königlich-Sächsische Coffee Service (1873–83)

The desire to go completely overboard with ornamentation and cover every square centimeter of this coffee set with designs inspired by nature may seem extreme, but we've always found extremism a rather juicy design strategy.

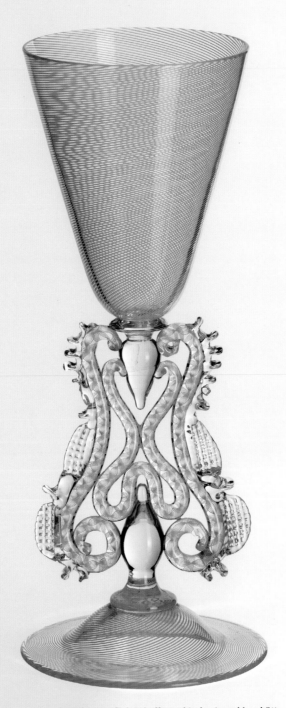

Winged Glass (1860) by Gräflich Schaffgotsch'sche Josephinenhütte
The company Josephinenhütte produced luxury items for the European courts, inspired
by the Venetian masters. Held in the collection of the Museum für Gestaltung in Zürich, this glass,
we assume, would markedly improve the taste of any wine.

Champagner Cup and Champagne Glasses from Service 126 and 145 (1865–75) by J. & L. Lobmeyr
No explanation needed here. They are simply glorious.

Cup Vase (1934–35) by Sven Erik Skawonius
A straightforward shape featuring a straightforward pattern.

Persian Koran (17th century)

Since Islamic artists were forbidden to depict realistic imagery, they focused their energy on calligraphy and ornament, making the Korans of seventeenth-century Persia arguably the most beautiful books ever created.

Still Life with a Chinese Porcelain Jar (1669) **by Willem Kalf**
Life literally stops in this still life from the golden era of Dutch painting.

Ring Monstrance
A monstrance represents the ultimate piece of display design: a receptacle that protects and showcases a consecrated object.

CRÉATION TEXTE & MUSIQUE JACQUES REBOTIER / MISE EN SCÈNE & SCÉNOGRAPHIE ÉRIC VIGNER / DIRECTION MUSICALE PHILIPP
ARRII-BLACHETTE / AVEC ARTHUR NAUZYCIEL, ISA LAGARDE, EVE PAYEUR, VINCENT THOMAS, DIDIER MEU, PHILIPPE ARRII
BLACHETTE, SÉBASTIEN ROUILLARD / ASSISTANT À LA MISE EN SCÈNE MATTHIAS SAILLARD / LUMIÈRES CHRISTOPHE DELARUE
SON FRÉDÉRIC LAÜGT / RÉGIE PLATEAU BRUNO ROBIN / VIDÉO MATTHIAS SAILLARD/BRUNO ROBIN PRODUCTION CDDB
CENTRE DRAMATIQUE DE BRETAGNE THÉÂTRE DE LORIENT / ASSOCIATION DRAMA/ENSEMBLE SILLAGES / LE QUARTZ, BRES
CDDB CENTRE DRAMATIQUE DE BRETAGNE THÉÂTRE DE LORIENT 11 RUE CLAIRE DRONEAU 56100 LORIENT TÉL 02 9783 515

5 REPRÉSENTATIONS DU ④ AU ⑩ MARS 1996

CDDB théâtre de LORIENT

Vigner

Rebotier

toi tour mon jardin

...

Toi cour moi jardin, CDDB and Théâtre de Lorient, Poster (1998) by M/M Paris

Michael Amzalag and Mathias Augustyniak of M/M Paris designed dozens of formally driven posters for theater, fashion, and music clients—they're also behind many of Björk's excellent graphics. This twenty-year-old poster for the Théâtre de Lorient still holds up well.

Wine Glass (c. 1907–10) by Otto Prutscher

A highly complex process was used to create a clean shape.

Children's Slippers (c. 1850)
You'd have to go to Jean Paul Gaultier to find house shoes for the kids even remotely as stylish
as these from the mid-nineteenth century.

Miss Alice Ladies' Hat (c. 1950)
Sadly, the hat has lost its place among must-have accessories for men and women. This stylish
concoction of laurels, forget-me-nots, violets, and white roses was sold in the United States under the "Miss Alice"
label, likely an homage to Lewis Carroll's equally wonderful *Alice's Adventures in Wonderland* (1865).

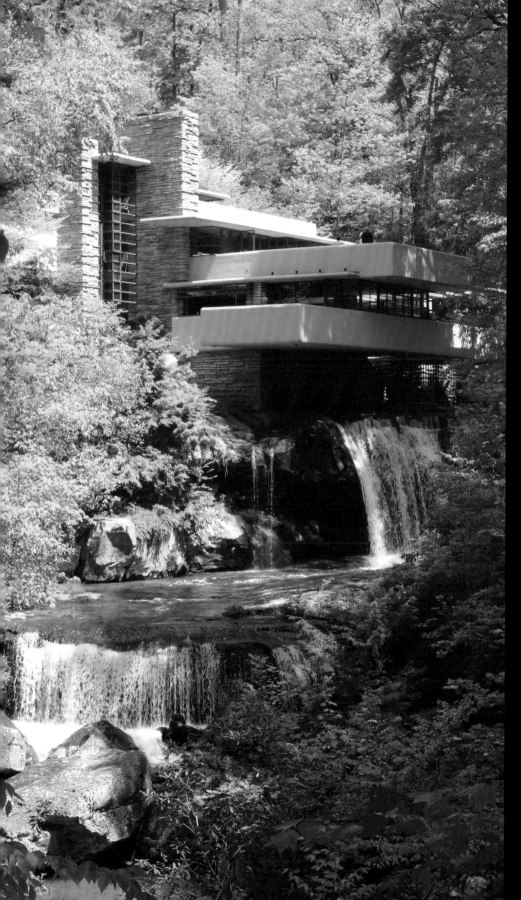

Fallingwater (1935) by Frank Lloyd Wright

Yes, yes, yes, we know, including such a classic in this list might seem a little banal. It's just that it is truly so good. Wright understood that his clean lines would work best when contrasted against the ruggedness of nature. The results are stunning and possibly even sublime.

Mughal Period Painting of Emperor Shahjahan (c. 1660–70)
The mixture of Persian and Indian styles beautifully combines naturalism in portraiture with floral ornament.

Float (2014) by United Nude with 3D Systems
United Nude, a company created by Rem D. Koolhaas and Galahad Clark, positions itself as a manufacturer of architectural footwear that meets at the intersection of design and fashion. In 2014, it launched a line of wearable 3-D printed shoes called Float, which could be printed at home.

Louis I and Louis II (2004) by Regula Dettwiler

A beautiful manifestation of the wonderfully naïve desire to improve on nature.

Willow Bough Wallpaper (1887) by William Morris

The tension between repetitive pattern and free-flowing nature elevates this British Arts and Crafts wallpaper to the world of high aesthetics. Andrew Grant Richardson created an animated version as a projection, where the branches grow steadily upward and the leaves shake subtly in the wind.

La Muralla Roja [The Red Wall] (1973) by Ricardo Bofill

La Muralla Roja is a housing complex designed by Bofill in the Spanish town of Calpe. Inspired by the architecture of coastal North Africa, the striking colors, staircases, and platforms are reminiscent of an M. C. Escher image of impossible architecture.

Lime-Basil Triangulation, from *Geometric Desserts* (2015–17) by Dinara Kasko
Kasko's background in architecture, design, and 3-D visualization influences her pastry art. These gorgeous geometric cakes (see also p. 230) are almost too beautiful to eat.

Stadthalle Chair (c. 1952) by Roland Rainer

Rainer designed this chair in the 1950s for the large Stadthalle concert hall in Vienna. Seventy years later, twelve of them provide us with beautiful seating in our meeting room in New York.

FORM OHNE ORNAMENT

AUSSTELLUNG

GEWERBEMUSEUM ZÜRICH

22.MÄRZ BIS 20.FEBRUAR

Räch

10.mai - 9.juni 1957   10 -12, 14-18
samstag/sonntag 10 -12, 14-17   montag nur 14-18

schallplattenhüllen aus amerika und europa
entwürfe junger schweizer grafiker

grammo-grafik   kunstgewerbemuseum zürich

Form ohne Ornament–Ausstellung–Gewerbemuseum Zürich Poster (1927) by Walter Käch

Influenced by the Austrian architect Adolf Loos's book *Ornament and Crime*, Käch's poster, "Form without Ornament," represents the perfectly efficient embodiment of the content it advertises.

Grammo-grafik, Kunstgewerbemuseum Zürich Poster (1957) by Gottlieb Soland

A reduced, down-to-the-basics, classic piece from the 1950s that has been copied countless times and still proves influential today.

La Grande Armoire d'Orphée Tapestry (1946) by Jean Lurçat

Imagine having the vague idea for an image of an open cabinet, granting a view of the outside, populated by all sorts of animals, and then saying, "That's it, let's painstakingly produce it as a wall-hanging." Lurçat clearly had the imagination and wherewithal to execute it. He wrote, "A tapestry is an object and, in its essence, a fabric, the purpose of which is to dress part of a building, for without this ornamentation it would no doubt lack a sense of body, passion, or quite frankly, charm."[1]

Seed Cathedral, UK Pavilion, Shanghai World Expo (2010) by Thomas Heatherwick

Even though it looks like an ethereal computer-generated rendering, it is, in fact, real.

Hair Design (2016) by Angelo Seminara
Seminara is one of the most influential hair designers of our time, having won numerous British Hairdresser of the Year awards.

Cup with Flowers (1910) designer unknown

The straightforward glass form and free-flowing flowers create a gorgeous tension.

**Fabrick (2015) by Somdatta Majumdar, Xixi Zheng, I-Ting Tsai, and Yiru Yun, with guidance
from Daniel Widrig, Soomeen Hahm, and Stefan Bassing**
Students at the Bartlett School of Architecture, University College London, used computer algorithms
to create a structurally sound chair out of a single flat sheet of felt material.
While the shape looks a bit alien, its symmetry and subtle shades of gray are oddly appealing.

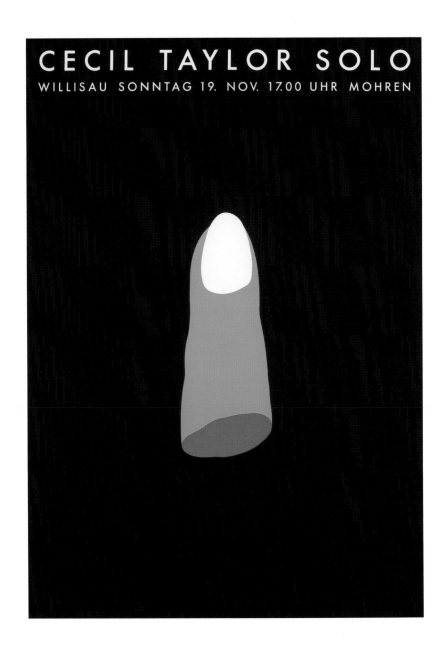

Cecil Taylor Solo Poster (1989) by Niklaus Troxler
Troxler enjoys one of the most unusual and remarkable careers in design. He founded the famous
Jazz Festival Willisau in Switzerland, and over the span of many decades, he designed its posters. Essentially
working for only a single client—himself—Troxler amassed a body of work unique in design history.
He was able to make a living for his family—all three of his talented daughters chose to become designers—
and he single-handedly put the village of Willisau on the cultural map.

MUSEUM FÜR GESTALTUNG ZÜRICH

SPORT DESIGN

13. NOVEMBER 2004–13. MÄRZ 2005

Sportdesign Poster for the Museum für Gestaltung Zürich (2004) by Martin Woodtli

Woodtli was already a full-fledged designer when he interned at our small studio in New York. Upon returning to Zürich, he immediately established himself as a true force within the Swiss design scene. We saw dozens of iterations he created before ending up with this formally sophisticated poster for an exhibit on sports.

Chair No. 4, then Standard Chair (1934) by Jean Prouvé

Prouvé's "Standard" chair is the result of a collaboration with Vitra. Conceived to be affordably mass-produced—in production from the 1930s to the early 1950s— this became one of Prouvé's most popular pieces.

TAC 1 Tea Set (product design, 1969; décor, 1979) by Walter Gropius, Louis McMillen, and Herbert Bayer
Three Bauhaus giants collaborated on a tea set that is fun, whimsical, and beautiful.
Gropius and McMillen designed the form, Bayer drew the decoration, and together they created a sense
of joy that is so sadly absent from many other Bauhaus pieces.

Villiger Export Poster (1937) by Johannes Handschin
Stefan wrote this while traveling: "I'm writing this text sitting in a goat herder's hut 20 km from the
Swiss border, smoking the exact same Villiger Export depicted on this 1937 poster. The price has increased
to SFr. 4.80 for a pack of five, but it tastes just as fine as it did almost eighty years ago." The design
has changed only to make room for the large government warning; the rest remains a testament to the notion
that when you design something well the first time around, it can remain the same.

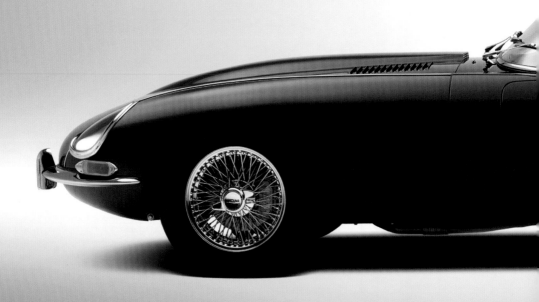

E-Type (1961–75) by Jaguar
Enzo Ferrari called this the most beautiful car of all time. He would know.

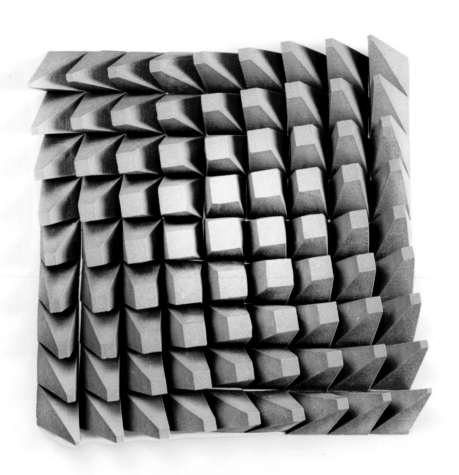

Algorithmic Modeling Cake, from *Geometric Desserts* (2015–17) by Dinara Kasko

One more of Kasko's delicious and gorgeous geometric pastries
(see also p. 211).

Hanairo Enpitsu (2017) by Toshihiro Otomo
Japanese designer Otomo transformed a boring object into something delightful: each pencil has
a unique flower shape that reveals its colorful petals when sharpened.

VitraHaus (2010) by Herzog & de Meuron

Our favorite of the star architecture firms, Herzog & de Meuron, came up with the ideal concept for what is essentially a furniture showroom. All of Vitra's home furniture can be presented inside a perfect, classic house structure. The intersections of the stacked houses, the various ways of moving from one floor to another, and the overall iconic shape form a near-perfect whole.

CAT 797F (2009)

The children's toy model of this giant mining dump truck is more famous than the original. To experience the real machine up close, its iconic shape and stupefying size, is awe-inspiring.

Chand Baori, Jaipur (c. 9th century)

Throughout Rajasthan, there are many stepwells, ancient water wells that are reached by descending a complex series of steps. With 3,500 steps and more than thirteen stories, Chand Baori, near Jaipur, is one of the most impressive. While the steps were built for utilitarian purposes, these Escher-esque wells are uniquely beautiful, especially when the light hits the steps, casting dramatic shadows.

The Bibliothèque Nationale de France (1368)

The Bibliothèque Nationale de France was founded as the royal library by Charles V. It's one of the largest libraries in the world, with more than forty million documents in its vast collections.

BUILT UP WITH STONES FALLEN DOWN FROM THE SKY
AUFGEBAUT MIT VOM HIMMEL GEFALLENEN STEINEN

Wherewithal / Was es Braucht (2016) by Lawrence Weiner

We usually prefer artists who embrace change to those who follow the same paths throughout their careers, but every once in a while we are happy to see somebody stick with one thing. Weiner's longtime use of outlined typography, which builds an imagined sculpture in the viewer's mind, is beautiful.

Mutual Vibration (2017) by Jonny Niesche

Humans are biologically hardwired to find sunsets beautiful, and they respond similarly to gradients. Niesche's abstract gradient pieces take advantage of this phenomenon; although simple, they are quite mesmerizing.

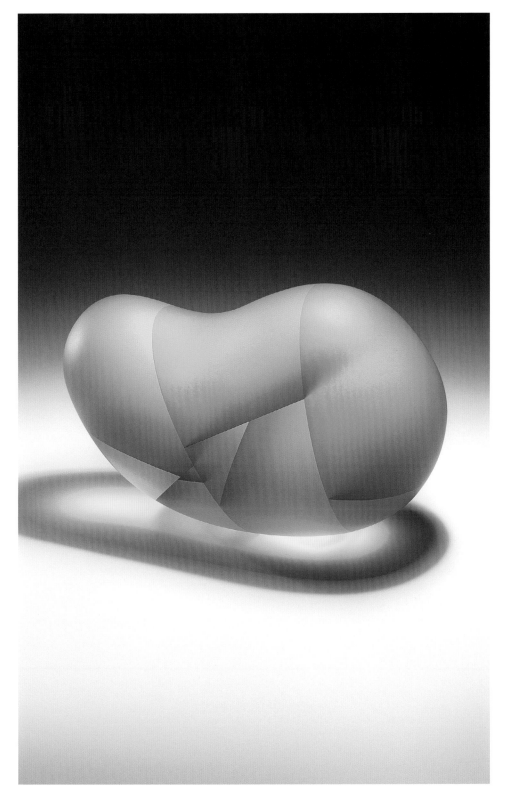

***Embryo Segmentation—Complexity of Life* (2011) by Jiyong Lee**

Lee's glass sculptures are not created from glassblowing or kilns but through a labor-intensive process of cutting, sanding, laminating, and carving. His attention to color and translucency, combined with meticulous craft, create a unique optical effect well worth his extensive effort.

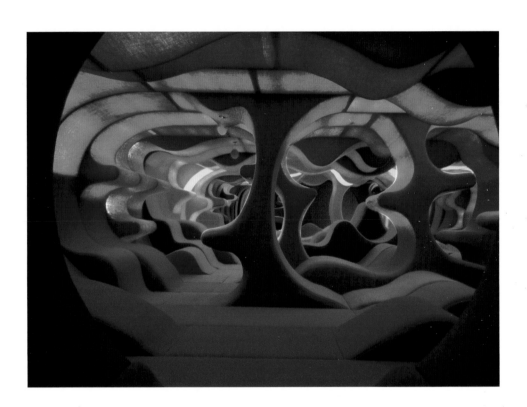

Interiors (1970) by Verner Panton
Panton is known for his iconic Panton Chair, but we always found his funky, psychedelic interiors for
restaurants and office spaces much more memorable.

The Peacock Room, Sammezzano Castle, Reggello, Italy (1605)
It's too bad that this more-than-four-hundred-year-old castle has been left abandoned for the last few decades, as it
would be a treat to spend time in any of its 365 elaborately decorated rooms—one for each day of the year.

Blur Building (2002) by Diller Scofidio + Renfro

The creation of a cloudlike building on a lake in Switzerland is a beautiful idea all by itself. The experience of walking through the structure, encountering various densities of fog, and sampling a wide selection of waters from around the world is gorgeous, too.

Hot with the Chance of Late Storm (2006) by the Glue Society
This melted ice-cream truck was a symbol for the Australian summer. It was shown on nearly every news show Down Under and became an icon for global warming.

<u>St. Peter's Basilica, Vatican City (1506–1615)</u>
As an atheist, Jessica usually avoids churches, but found it hard to leave St. Peter's Basilica
on her recent trip to Italy. Every inch of the Renaissance architecture is covered in works by the masters,
including Gian Lorenzo Bernini, Donato Bramante, Michelangelo, and Raphael.

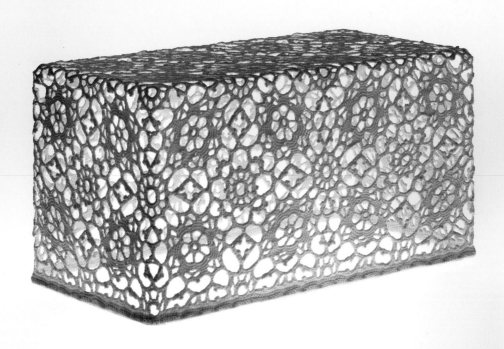

Crochet Side Table (2001) by Marcel Wanders
A modernist form perfectly executed through a combination of nineteenth-century craft and contemporary
technology, this table is constructed from individual, hand-crocheted flowers that are formed
over a mold and stiffened with resin. It was offered at a Moss auction in New York paired with a historic portrait
depicting a woman in a crocheted dress.[2] Perfection.

Frühlingsfahrten [Driving through Spring] (1945) by Donald Brun

A jumping lamb forming a cloud in the sky constitutes a formidable symbol for a drive through spring. In the 1950s and '60s, Brun replaced the then-popular beautiful woman at the center of many commercial pieces with various animals. Next to Herbert Leupin, he was arguably the most important Swiss poster designer of his time.

Mirrorcube Treehotel (2010) by Tham & Videgård Arkitekter

Designed by Tham & Videgård forty miles south of the Arctic Circle in Sweden, this eco-hotel was built with a lightweight aluminum structure wrapped in mirrored glass and supported by a tree trunk in the center.

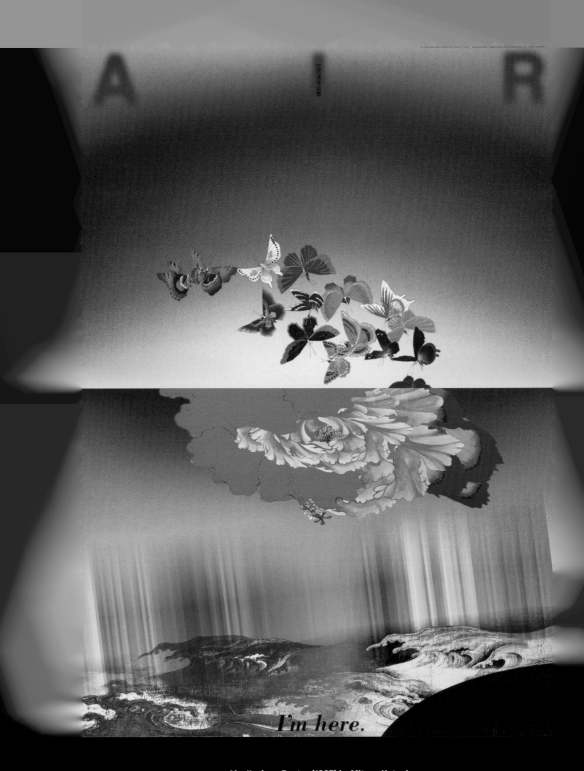

Air–I'm here Poster (1993) by Mitsuo Katsui

In our opinion, Japan might be the only first-world country where the pursuit of beauty in design was not eliminated during the twentieth century. Japanese masters such as Katsui pursued beauty unapologetically; here, he draws on his ability to create contemporary work even while relying on clichés such as butterflies, waves, and flowers.

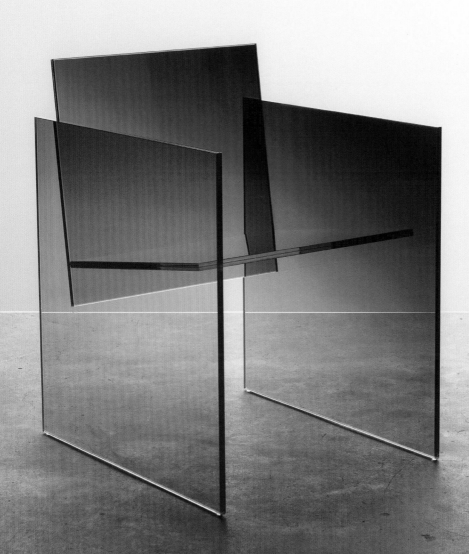

Ombré Glass Chair (2017) by Germans Ermičs

The Ombré Glass Chair was created by Latvian-born designer Ermičs as a tribute to Shiro Kuramata's iconic Glass Chair.

Amber Fort, Jaipur, India (16th century)

Another beautiful spot from Jessica's Rajasthan travels: three windows carved with a repeating geometric pattern cast a gorgeous light inside Amber Fort conservatory in Jaipur.

Jardin Majorelle (1923–61) by Jacques Majorelle

French painter Majorelle spent nearly forty years creating this garden in Marrakech. The greens of the plants pop against the cobalt-blue and pure-yellow paint of the cubist villa, which was designed by French architect Paul Sinoir and later purchased by Yves Saint Laurent and Pierre Bergé.

Tulip Stairs, Queen's House, Greenwich, England (1635) by Inigo Jones

Jones designed this breathtaking staircase to follow the Fibonacci sequence—a numerical pattern found in mathematics, art, architecture, and nature. The mathematical ideas behind the sequence have long been appreciated for their beauty.

Swiss Currency (issued 1995–98) by Jörg Zintzmeyer

We have long been fans of the (now old) Swiss currency and own a complete set signed by its designer, the late Jörg Zintzmeyer. It is said to have included sixteen different security features, some known only to the Swiss National Bank. The vertical direction, the decision to depict only artists as subjects, as well as the absolutely impeccable printing technique make this our favorite currency in the world. No other mint could even attempt to print it—it would be just too difficult to stay within tolerances that small.

Three-Legged Chair (1949) by Max Bill

It might be a bit shaky, but this three-legged version of Bill's more popular four-legged Cross-Frame Chair
is much better looking. Note how the back leg gracefully extends to support the backrest.
Bill gave an important lecture in which he proclaimed that function alone can never lead to good work—
beauty must be equally prioritized.[3]

Amaltea 1986   Pasifila 1986

Corinna 1986   Ananke 1986

Memphis Milano (1982–86) by Ettore Sottsass

Italian architect and designer Sottsass's colorful and playful work has been described as "bizarre" and "atrocious." Perhaps there is something wrong with our eyes, but we find it quite lovely; these would be welcome additions to our homes.

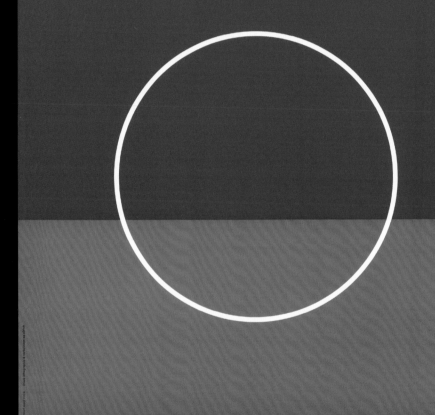

dc7c Panair do Brasil Poster (1957) by Mary Vieira

The perfect symmetry broken by the asymmetrical horizon creates a quiet tension
that still vibrates sixty years later.

Adjustable Garden Chair (date below) by Werner Max Moser
Without looking at the date, when do you think this lovely, adjustable garden chair was designed: in the 1950s? 1960s?
It was created in 1931, when this kind of minimalist form was truly innovative. Moser worked in
Frank Lloyd Wright's studio and was one of the architects for Ludwig Mies van der Rohe's apartment block
in the Weissenhofsiedlung [Weissenhof Estate] in Stuttgart.

Glass Kugeldose (1925) by Oswald Haerdtl (design) and J. & L. Lobmeyr (manufacturing)
Another missive from Stefan's travels: "I have admired this glass in the windows of J. & L. Lobmeyr on Kärntner
Straße in Vienna for a long time; they still manufacture this masterpiece in various sizes today.
Designed originally for the 1925 Exposition Internationale des Arts Décoratifs in Paris, this piece is a perfect
example of a reduced-to-the-max depiction of nature."

1. Jean Lurçat, <u>Le travail dans la tapisserie du Moyen-Âge</u> (Genève: Cailler, 1947). « La tapisserie, c'est principalement chose d'architecture...c'est un objet et dans son essence un tissu, dont le devoir est d'habiller un pan de bâtiment à qui, sans cet ornement, eût sans doute manqué un je-ne-sais-quoi de charnu, de passionnel, de charme pour tout dire. »

2. Moss was a design store in New York run by Murray Moss. During its heyday, it was the best design store in the world; now it's sadly closed.

3. Max Bill, "Beauty from Function and as Function," in <u>Form, Function, Beauty = Gestalt</u>, Architecture Words 5 (London: Architectural Association Publications, 2010), 34. See the German original: "Schönheit aus Funktion und als Funktion," <u>Werk</u> 36, no. 8 (1949): 272-74.

Pt. —

The Bea

VII

Project

The Beauty Project:

A Manifesto

WE believe that beauty itself is function. Without it, nothing ever really works well. As designers, we must never forget how important beauty is to our work, or we'll be condemned to a world in which expediency is privileged and dull work predominates. As we've observed, beauty raises both the standards for creativity and its results. By aiming higher than the simply utilitarian solution, we achieve more. We believe design and beauty can improve people's lives. There's much to be done to increase beauty in the world, and in the lives of people who particularly need it. Our desire to use design to improve communities is what drives us. We present this chapter as our strategy for further action.

1

We are committed to "The Beauty Project," the single
goal of which is to translate the arguments and findings of this
book into our daily lives.

2

When we talk about beauty, we're talking about formal intent.

3

Pretty is never enough. Useful is never enough.

4

We ask others to join us and begin their own efforts to further
this initiative.

5

We will identify neglected areas in cities and develop smart
strategies to infuse them with beauty.

6

We pledge to be inclusive, to work with a broad range
of communities, knowing that beauty plays an indisputable
social role in all of our lives, influencing how we feel
and how we act, and everyone should benefit. Beauty comes
from reach and outreach.

7

We will target spaces that are considered ugly, overlooked,
and ignored.

8

Design can create beauty for everyone, everywhere.

Thank You

We would like to thank our wonderful designers at Sagmeister & Walsh—Daniel Brokstad, Shy Inbar, Matteo Giuseppe Pani, Bika Sibila Rebek, and Chen Yu—for helping us create this book, as well as the exhibition on beauty.

All the heavy design lifting was done by the fantastic Kevin Brainard, Cybele Grandjean, and Tala Safié of Area of Practice. Thank you so much for your expertise and never-ending patience.

This considerable amount of work would never have come together properly without our fantastic producer, Erica Grubman, who was supported by Megan Oldfield and Gosbinda Vizarretea.

270

The text was improved steadily by Sara Hamilton and our editors at Phaidon, the terrific Deborah Aaronson and Sara Bader, who never tired of correcting our sloppy thinking and terrible grammar. We are thankful to Elaine Ward and Alenka Oblak for their production support. Anne Ray expertly copyedited the text, Lindsey Westbrook diligently proofread it, and Aude Devanthéry fact-checked the manuscript. Thanks to photo researchers Romayne Gadelrab and Ting-Yu Tsen, and Alex Brovkin for adding up the numbers of our surveys.

Bertram Schmidt-Friderichs at our German publisher, Verlag Hermann Schmidt, organized a first-rate translation of the manuscript.

We are also grateful to all the people who organized our lectures on beauty around the world. These talks allowed us to try out different themes and bring some degree of focus to this vast and elusive subject.

This book is supported by an exhibition on beauty coproduced by two excellent museums, the Museum of Applied Arts (MAK) in Vienna and the Museum Angewandte Kunst Frankfurt am Main. At the MAK Vienna, Rainald Franz, Martina Kandeler-Fritsch, Sebastian Hackenschmidt, Teresa Marchesani, Kathrin Pokorny-Nagel, Elisabeth Schmuttermeier, Christoph Thun-Hohenstein, Bärbel Vische, Johannes Wieninger, Marlies Wirth, and architect Michael Wallraff were instrumental in the making of the exhibition. Thank you also to Dr. Rainald Franz, the curator for glass and ceramics who helped select the historic glasses.

At the Museum Angewandte Kunst Frankfurt am Main our thanks go out to Matthias Wagner K and Peter Zizka.

We are grateful to Swarovski AG in Wattens, Austria, for the exhibition collaboration and the generous support. We are also indebted to the lovely Jonathan Levine at Master & Dynamic for installing a complete sound room.

Stefan would like to thank his sisters—Andrea, Christine, and Veronika— and his brothers—Gebhard and Martin—for their tremendous support and for giving him, despite his having lived in New York for almost thirty years, the feeling that he is still properly rooted in the ground.

Jessica would like to thank her family for their endless love and support: Sarah and Joe Walsh, Lauren Walsh, Zak Mulligan, and last but not least, Oscar Mulligan-Walsh (her dog).